2nd EDITION

INCREDIBLE ENGLISH

Class Book

6

MW01142914

Sarah Phillips

Peter Redpath

OXFORD
UNIVERSITY PRESS

1 Listen and read. 🔊 1.1

THE NATIONAL CHALLENGE

1 The National Challenge begins.

This is our big day. We're in the National Challenge.

Look. Perhaps that's another team.

Yes, perhaps. There are three other teams in the finals.

2 Good morning, teams. I'm the supervisor. Please follow my assistant.

Hi, kids. Your team names and team colours are ready. Come with me.

3 Hello.

Hi.

We're the Incredible Reds.

We're the Cool Greens.

4 This is the Brilliant Yellow Team and the Excellent Blue Team.

Ladies and gentlemen. The National Challenge teams!

5 OK, teams! It's time to meet the Press!

I've never been in a newspaper before.

6

2 Look at the story and answer the questions. 📝

1 How many teams are there in the National Challenge?

2 What are the teams' names?

3 What is Meg's team called?

4 Who do the teams meet at the end?

5 Who is the woman in blue?

1 Read and match the questions to the paragraphs.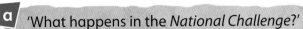

a 'What happens in the *National Challenge*?'

b 'What do they do when they have got the answer?'

c 'How do they find the answer?'

d 'How does the competition end?'

e 'Can you tell me about the teams?'

The National Challenge!

The *National Challenge* started today. Our reporter, Nick Jones, talked to Sarah, the supervisor.

1

'There are four teams, the Incredible Reds, the Cool Greens, the Excellent Blues and the Brilliant Yellows. They all won their local competitions.'

2

'There are nine questions. We travel to different places on a bus. We are going to go to a nature park, a planetarium, a concert, a theme park and lots of other exciting places. The teams will meet a famous actor and a famous rockstar. They get the question on their mobiles when they arrive at the challenge.'

3

'They have to work together as a team. They have to use their eyes and ears, and most importantly, they have to think.'

4

'The team leaders call me on their mobile phones. The first team to call gets four points, the second team gets three points, the third team gets two points and the last team gets one point.'

5

'That's a secret. Follow the *National Challenge* and see!'

2 Answer the questions.

1 How many teams are there in the National Challenge?
2 Why are these teams in the National Challenge?
3 How many questions are there?
4 When do the teams get their questions?
5 What is the most important thing the teams have to do?
6 Who do the teams call with the answer to the question?

3 Listen and say which team.  1.2

The Excellent Blue Team

The Brilliant Yellow Team

The Incredible Red Team

The Cool Green Team

team members	Meg Harris Oli Clark Rav Kotecha	Mike Smith Kate Thompson Tom Ash	Jen Wilson Emma Green Matt Wood	Amy Turner Bev Dilks Mark Ball
school	Castleford School	Newbridge School	Southport School	Eastgate School
good at	problem solving	sport and team games	trekking and mountain climbing	music, dance and art
winners of	Castleford chess tournament	Under 13s swimming cup	Southport cross-country race	National hip hop championships
been to	a planetarium	a theme park	a nature park	a concert
met	a rock star	a famous actor	a rock star	a famous actor

4 Answer the questions.

1 Who's in the Red Team?
2 What school do the Red Team go to?
3 What's the Red Team good at?
4 Have the Red Team ever won a chess tournament?
5 Have the Red Team ever been to a theme park?

5 Now ask your partner about the other teams.

What's the Blue Team good at?

Trekking and mountain climbing.

1 At the nature park

1 Look, listen and repeat. 🔘 1.3

landscape

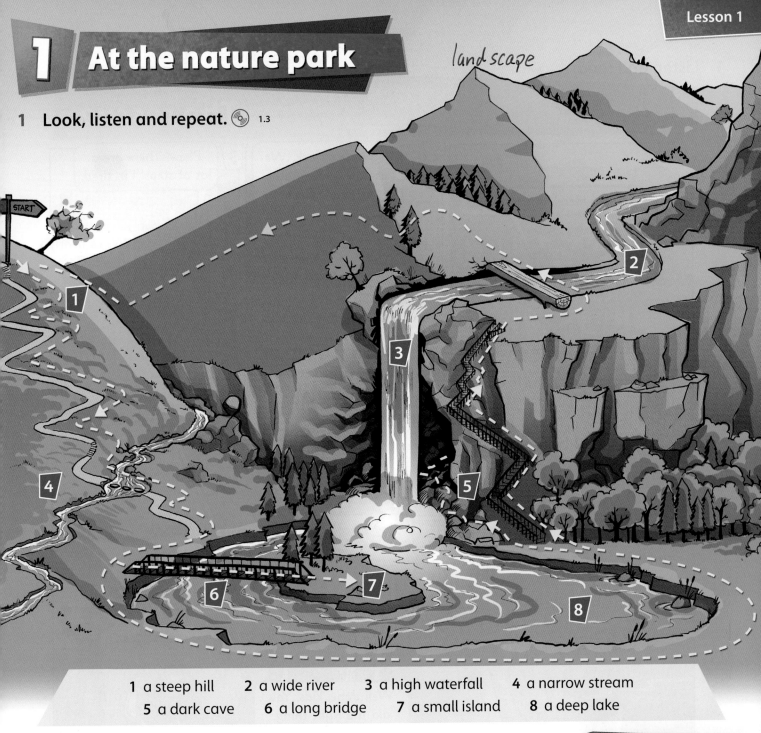

START

1 | 2 | 3 | 4 | 5 | 6 | 7 | 8

1 a steep hill   2 a wide river   3 a high waterfall   4 a narrow stream
5 a dark cave   6 a long bridge   7 a small island   8 a deep lake

2 Look and correct the words in blue. 📝

1 The walk starts at the top of a <u>deep lake</u>.
2 The walk goes down the hill and then crosses a <u>high waterfall</u>.
3 The waterfall falls into a wide river.
4 The bridge goes across the lake to a dark cave.
5 There is a dark cave behind a narrow stream.
6 At the top of the steps there is a small island.

3 Point to the picture. Ask and answer.

What's the hill like?

It's steep.

What's the river like?

It's wide.

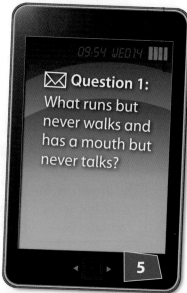

09:54 WED 14

✉ **Question 1:**
What runs but never walks and has a mouth but never talks?

5

1 Listen and read. 1.6

2   Look and say. Which sentences are in the story?

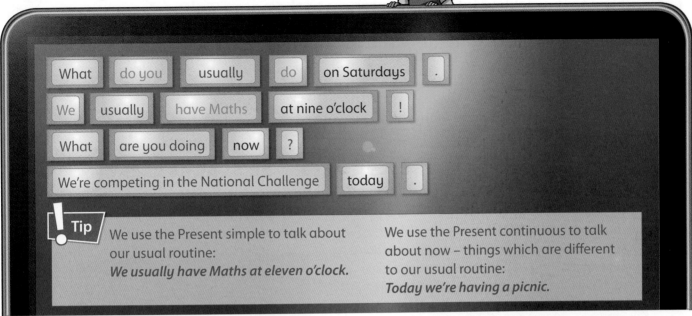

| What | do you | usually | do | on Saturdays | . |

| We | usually | have Maths | at nine o'clock | ! |

| What | are you doing | now | ? |

| We're competing in the National Challenge | today | . |

> **! Tip**
> We use the Present simple to talk about our usual routine:
> *We usually have Maths at eleven o'clock.*
>
> We use the Present continuous to talk about now – things which are different to our usual routine:
> *Today we're having a picnic.*

3   Look at the pictures and finish the dialogue.

It's Saturday at the nature park.

What's she doing today?

She's fishing in the lake.

What does she usually do on Saturdays?

She usually plays tennis.

Number **Z** ?

Yes!

4   Listen and repeat. 1.7

What's she doing today?

She's fishing in the lake.

What does she usually do on Saturdays?

She usually plays tennis.

5   Choose a different picture. Make questions and answers.

What	's she doing today	?	She's
fishing in the lake	climbing a hill	exploring a cave
.	What	does she	usually	do
on Saturdays	?	She	usually	plays tennis
does her homework	visits her grandparents	.

6   Complete the grammar table.

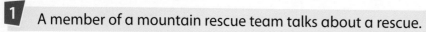

Mountain rescue is difficult and dangerous! Read the article.

1 Read the text quickly. Match the sentences to the paragraphs.

1 A member of a mountain rescue team talks about a rescue.

2 A person who was lost on a mountain talks about a rescue.

3 We need Mountain Rescue teams because walking on mountains can be dangerous.

MOUNTAIN RESCUE HEROES

a Every weekend hundreds of people go walking in the hills and mountains in Britain. Sometimes the weather is bad and walkers <u>get lost</u>. Sometimes climbers have <u>accidents</u> and can't move. Sometimes walkers don't arrive home. Every weekend the Mountain Rescue teams have to help people who get into trouble.

b **My name's Claire Noakes.** I work with the Mountain Rescue team in Wales. We were looking for some students last winter. We knew they were on the mountain but we couldn't find them. It was dark and foggy, we couldn't see more than five metres. We were very <u>worried</u>. Suddenly I saw a flash of light, then another and another. One of the students had a good idea. He was taking pictures with his mobile phone.

He wanted to attract our attention with the flash. We followed the flashes and found the students. They were very cold, but they were all alright.

c **My name's Jenny Brown.** I was hiking in the hills with a friend last summer. My friend fell down and hurt her ankle. We started to go down the mountain, but we had to go very slowly. Then the sun <u>set</u> and it got cold. We didn't have jumpers or anoraks and soon we were <u>shivering</u>. We didn't have any food and we were very hungry. But worst of all, we couldn't see anything. I was really scared. Luckily my friend had a mobile phone. She called the rescue team. At about two in the morning I heard a dog <u>barking</u>. It was Blackie, a mountain rescue dog. Blackie and the Mountain Rescue team helped us down the mountain.

2 Complete the sentences with words from the text.

1 At the end of the day the sun went down. It _____ .

2 I had two _____ when I was skiing. First I broke my leg and then I broke my arm.

3 The dog saw the cat and he started _____ .

4 It is easy to _____ when it is foggy.

5 I was very cold. I couldn't stop moving, and I was *shivering*

6 'I can't find my dog, I'm very *worried*.'

3 Read the text again and answer the questions.

1 What sometimes happens to people in the mountains?

2 What does Claire do?

3 Who were they looking for?

4 Why couldn't Claire's team find them?

5 What did Claire see?

6 What was Jenny doing in the hills?

7 What happened?

8 Why did she feel scared?

9 Who rescued them?

1 Match the pictures to the sentences.

d 1 Take some chocolate and water.

c 2 Wear the right clothes.

f 3 Tell someone where you are going and what time you are returning.

e 4 Take a map, a compass, a whistle and a torch.

h 5 Put on sun cream.

g 6 Be careful: don't walk on snow or ice, don't cross full streams.

a 7 Check the weather forecast and monitor the weather.

b 8 Take a mobile phone.

2 Listen. Which safety points do they talk about? Write the letters in order. 🎧 1.13

a . c . b . e , d

3 Listen again and choose the right answer. 🎧 1.13

1 Who is Mr Price?
   (a) a member of the Rescue team   **b** a hiker   **c** the radio presenter

2 What kinds of weather were there last Sunday?
   a sun and rain   **b** rain and snow   **(c)** sun and snow

3 What clothes does Mr Price suggest for a warm day?
   a boots, T–shirt, anorak   **(b)** boots, cap, anorak   **c** trainers, cap, anorak

4 What should you take to call for help?
   a only a mobile phone   **(b)** a mobile phone and a whistle   **c** only a whistle

5 What food does Mr Price suggest?
   a chocolate and juice   **b** cereal bars and water   **(c)** chocolate and water

4 Listen and find the missing words. 🎧 1.14

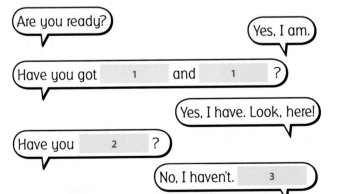

Are you ready?

Yes, I am.

Have you got   1   and   1 ?

Yes, I have. Look, here!

Have you   2 ?

No, I haven't.   3

What about   4 ?

Oh no! I forgot!

1   a whistle an anorak   a mobile phone a jumper

2   planned your route charged the phone   checked the weather

3   Good idea! Good thinking!

4   some biscuits some water   some chocolate

5 Do the role play with your partner. Choose different words.

Rivers

1 **Look, listen and repeat.** 🎧 1.15

2 **Listen, read and follow the course of the river.** 🎧 1.16

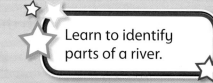

Learn to identify parts of a river.

Rivers are important. They give us food, energy, transport routes, water for agriculture, water for drinking and places to do sports.

This is the upper course of a river. It is called a stream. Streams are narrow and shallow. The water is clean and it runs fast. Streams often have waterfalls.

This is the middle course of a river. It is wider and deeper than a stream. The water moves more slowly and it is usually transparent.

upper course

middle course

stream

hydroelectric plant

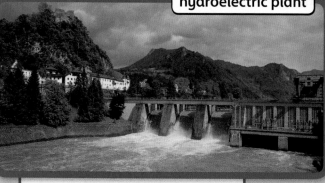

Hydroelectric plants use water to make electricity.

factory

Some factories need a lot of water and they are often built near rivers. The waste water from factories is sometimes dirty and pollutes the river.

3 **Read the text again and answer the questions.**

1 Name three things rivers provide.

2 What's the water like in the upper course of a river?

3 What does a hydroelectric plant do?

4 How does the water move in the middle course of a river?

5 What are three things people often build near rivers?

6 Why are factories built near rivers?

7 Why are bridges important?

8 Why do you find farms near the lower course of rivers?

9 What do you often find near very deep water?

River features

1 Listen. Find the photos and answer the questions. 1.18

This is the lower course of a river. The river is very wide, the water flows slowly and it is cloudy. Sometimes the water flows over the banks of the river. This is called a flood. Plants grow well on flood plains and so there are often farms on the lower course of a river.

lower course

water sports centre

There are water sports centres on rivers. You can go swimming, sailing and windsurfing.

bridge

You often find towns near rivers. People built bridges at points on the river where it was easy to cross. Bridges are important for communication, transport and business. People built villages near bridges and the villages grew into towns.

This is the mouth of a river. When the mouth of a river is deep you often find a port. Ships can sail into them.

flood plains

port

🗨 Talk about it!

2 Talk about the river.

What's this?   It's a hydroelectric plant.
Where is it?   It's on the upper course of a river.
What's the water like?   It's clean.
                                        It runs fast.

1 **Guess the missing words.** **Listen to the song and check.** 1.19

Song

We're catching   walk   stay   We're doing   have   visit
We're doing   lighting   swimming

It's Saturday today and we're all doing something new
We usually **1** home and try to think of things to do. _walk_
We often **2** _visit_ Grandma by the sea
We usually **3** cakes and cups of tea, but now …

We're all camping in a nature park
4 _fish and_ **5** _fires in the dark._
6 _something we don't usually do,_
7 _something that's different and new!_

We usually **8** in the park outside our school,
But today we're hiking and climbing and **9** in a pool. _swimming_
It's usually quite boring, yes it's true,
But today is really different and new, because …

2 **Play the game.**

How to play

- Play in two teams of two.
- You need six paper counters each. **Team 1:** write _1_ on your counters. **Team 2:** write _2_ on your counters.
- Put a counter on the board. You can put it on the bottom row, or above another counter.
- Read and do.
- The first team to make a line of **three** is the winner.

Talk about the picture on page 5 of your Class Book.	Tell the story of the students Claire Noakes rescued.	Make sentences from the words in Activity 5 on page 7 of your Class Book.	Describe the three parts of a river.
What happens in _The rescue?_	Where do you find factories on a river? Where do you find water sports centres? Why?	Sing the song _It's Saturday today …_	What happened to Jenny Brown?
Ask and answer about some natural features in your area.	Say the chant _I'm sitting on the steps of a cave near a lake._	What do Mountain Rescue teams do?	Do a role play with a friend: you are going walking in the mountains.

2 At the theme park

1 Look, listen and repeat. 🔊 1.20

1 a waterslide   2 a roller coaster   3 a big wheel   4 a prize   5 a bouncy castle
6 candyfloss   7 a toffee apple   8 bumper cars   9 a merry-go-round

2 Look and correct the words in blue. 📝

1 Two boys are buying candyfloss.
2 The two girls on the big wheel are eating candyfloss.
3 There is a boy on the roller coaster wearing a pink hat.
4 Two women are in a blue bumper car.
5 A boy is on a horse on the merry-go-round.
6 There are four people on the waterslide.
7 A man is buying a toffee apple.
8 The bouncy castle is red.

3 Point to the picture. Ask and answer.

Where is he?

He's on the big wheel.

Where are they?

They're on the roller coaster.

09:54 WED 14

✉ Question 2:
Go on the highest ride. How many towers has the castle got?

Theme park words

Lesson 2 ➔ AB page 13

1   Listen and read. 🎧 1.23

2 Look and say. Which sentence is in the story?

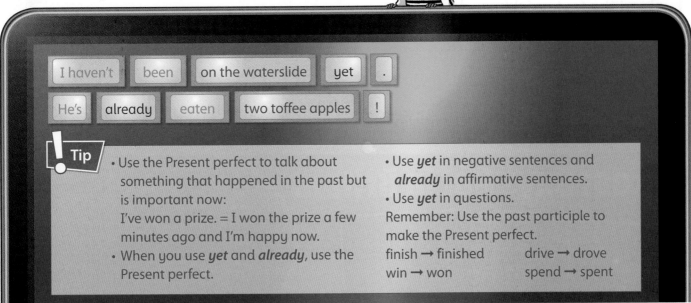

I haven't | been | on the waterslide | yet | .

He's | already | eaten | two toffee apples | !

Tip
- Use the Present perfect to talk about something that happened in the past but is important now:
  I've won a prize. = I won the prize a few minutes ago and I'm happy now.
- When you use *yet* and *already*, use the Present perfect.
- Use *yet* in negative sentences and *already* in affirmative sentences.
- Use *yet* in questions.
Remember: Use the past participle to make the Present perfect.
finish → finished   drive → drove
win → won   spend → spent

3 Look at the pictures and finish the dialogue.

Can you guess which boy?
He's already been on the waterslide.
He hasn't been on the roller coaster yet.
He's already eaten his toffee apple.
He hasn't eaten his candyfloss yet.

Yes!   Number ___ ?

4 Listen and repeat. 1.24

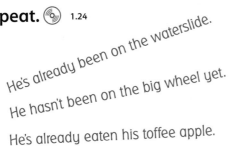

He's already been on the waterslide.
He hasn't been on the big wheel yet.
He's already eaten his toffee apple.
He hasn't eaten his candyfloss yet.

5 Choose a different boy. Make four sentences.

He's | already | eaten | been
on the roller coaster | on the waterslide
his toffee apples | his candyfloss | .
He hasn't | yet | .

6 Complete the grammar table.

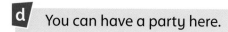
Read about great days out! Look at the leaflet!

1 Read the text quickly and say where.

a You can have a shower here.

b You can see lizards here.

c You can see Buckingham Palace from here.

d You can have a party here.

e You can travel at 100 kph here.

f You can see rainforest plants here.

Great Days Out in Britain

The London Eye: Visit the London Eye – it's London's most popular tourist attraction! It is 135 metres high and turns at 0.9 kph. Passengers get into a <u>capsule</u> and travel slowly round for 30 minutes. From the <u>top</u> of the wheel you can see Buckingham Palace, St Paul's Cathedral, the River Thames and some of London's parks. The London Eye isn't only for tourists, you can have a party in a capsule, and you can get married in one too!

The Eden Project: See the world in five hours! The Eden Project is a very special theme park in Cornwall. There aren't any rides, but there are enormous futuristic domes, called biomes, each one with a different <u>climate</u>. You can go from a tropical island, to a rainforest, to a desert, in a day. You can see thousands of plants as well as birds, insects and lizards.

Try following the food trail in the tropical dome and see bananas, <u>pineapples</u>, cocoa, coffee and the sapodilla tree (chewing gum is made from sapodilla sap).

Alton Towers: Come to Alton Towers, an enormous theme park with rides and attractions for <u>everyone</u>. Young children can drive tractors and play with soft balls in Old MacDonald's Farm. There are five different roller coasters, including Rita – Queen of Speed, which goes at 100 kph.

Try the water attractions! You can get in a boat and go down <u>rapids</u> and waterfalls! Or go on the Flume - it's like an enormous bathroom with baths, rubber ducks and showers too!

2 Find these words in the text.

1 highest point

2

3

4 all the people

5 weather conditions

6

7 the milky liquid inside plants

3 Read the text again and answer the questions.

1 Is the London Eye very popular?

2 Does the London Eye travel fast?

3 Are there any rides at the Eden Project?

4 Can you see any animals at the Eden Project?

5 Does chewing gum come from a plant?

6 Who can drive tractors at Alton Towers?

7 Does Rita go very fast?

8 Are there water attractions at Alton Towers?

1 **Listen and point to the photos.** 🎧 1.30

2 **Listen again and choose the right answer.** 🎧 1.30

1 Where does Tom sit?
   a in a tree   **b** on a leaf   **c** on a drum

2 What does the durian fruit smell like?
   a old socks   **b** goats   **c** bad eggs

3 What does the bee man teach you?
   a to make honey   **b** to make a bee picture   **c** to do a bee dance

4 What are the pig sculptures made of?
   a olive branches   **b** oak branches   **c** palm tree branches

5 What can you hear in the Tropical Biome?
   a African animals   **b** African drummers   **c** African songs

3 **Listen and find the missing words.** 🎧 1.31

Where did you go **1** ?

We went to **2** .

What did you like best?

 3

Why? What did you do there?

We **4** !

 5

1 at the weekend   last week   on your holidays

2 Cornwall   London   England

3 The Eden Project.   The London Eye.   Alton Towers.

4 saw a bee sculpture   had a party   went on the roller coasters

5 Brilliant!   That sounds fun.   That's interesting!

4 **Do the role play with your partner. Choose different words.**

Charts and graphs

1 **Look, listen and repeat.** 🔊 1.32

2 **Listen, read and answer.** 🔊 1.33

We find information everywhere: in books, in newspapers, on television and on the internet. When the information is numbers, we often put it into charts and graphs. This organizes the numbers and makes them easier to understand. Look at these charts and graphs about Megapark on the 15th of October.

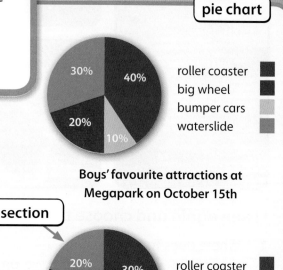

pie chart

roller coaster
big wheel
bumper cars
waterslide

Boys' favourite attractions at Megapark on October 15th

These are pie charts. They are useful when you are comparing two sets of data.

These pie charts show boys' and girls' favourite attractions. Each section represents a different attraction and is a different colour.

What colour represents the roller coaster?

The label on each section shows the percentage of the circle it represents. For example, 40% of the boys say the roller coaster is their favourite attraction.

What percentage of girls say the roller coaster is their favourite attraction?

section

roller coaster
big wheel
bumper cars
waterslide

Girls' favourite attractions at Megapark on October 15th

bar chart

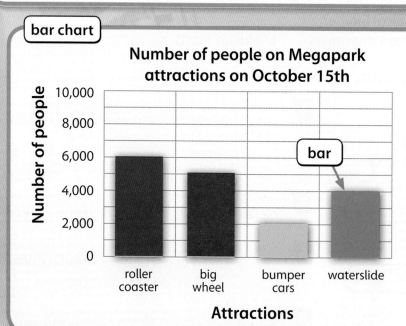

Number of people on Megapark attractions on October 15th

Number of people

10,000
8,000
6,000
4,000
2,000
0

roller coaster | big wheel | bumper cars | waterslide

bar

Attractions

This is a bar chart. We use bar charts to compare different groups. Each bar represents one group or thing.

This bar chart shows how many people went on some of the attractions.

Which attractions does it compare?

line graph

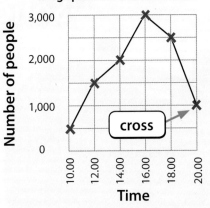

Number of people at Megapark on October 15th

Number of people / Time

cross

This is a line graph. We often use line graphs to show how things change at different times.

This line graph shows how the number of people at Megapark changed from opening time at 10 a.m. to closing time at 8 p.m. The crosses show the number of people at different times.

The line shows how the numbers go up and down.

When were there most people at Megapark?

pictogram

Ice creams sold at Megapark on October 15th

Ice cream flavour: chocolate, vanilla, strawberry, lemon, coffee

Number of ice creams

This is a pictogram. It uses symbols to show numbers of items.

This pictogram shows how many ice creams were eaten at Megapark. One ice cream symbol represents 100 ice creams.

What was the most popular ice cream?

symbol → = 100 ice creams

---

1   Look at the charts and make sentences.

1	40% of the boys	a	went on the bumper cars.
2	20% of the girls	b	bought chocolate ice creams.
3	5,000 people	c	in the park at 12 o'clock.
4	2,000 people	d	liked the roller coaster best.
5	There were 1,500 people	e	went on the big wheel.
6	There were 2,500 people	f	bought lemon ice creams.
7	1,000 people	g	liked the waterslide best.
8	300 people	h	in the park at 6 o'clock.

2   Listen, answer and check. 1.34

Talk about it!

3   Talk about graphs and charts.

Do more boys or girls like the bumper cars?

What is the boys' least favourite attraction?

How many people went on the roller coaster?

How many people were in the park at twelve o'clock?

Were there more people in the park at twelve o'clock or at two o'clock?

How many vanilla ice creams did they sell?

Did they sell more strawberry or lemon ice creams?

1 Guess the missing words. **Listen to the song and check.** 1.35

Song

haven't   already   seen   yet   already

Now we've **1** been on some of the rides,
The merry-go-round and the water slide.
We **2** seen the view from the top,
The big wheel's next – we just can't stop!

We haven't been on the water jet **3** *,*
And when we do, we're going to get wet,
wet, wet!

Yes, we've **4** been on some of the rides,
The roller coaster and the waterslide.
And now we've **5** the view from the top,
The bumper cars next – we just can't stop!

2 Play the game.

How to play
- Play in two teams of two.
- You need six paper counters each. **Team 1:** write *1* on your counters. **Team 2:** write *2* on your counters.
- Put a counter on the board. You can put it on the bottom row, or above another counter.
- Read and do.
- The first team to make a line of **three** is the winner.

Talk about the picture on page 13 of your Class Book.	Talk about The London Eye and Alton Towers.	Make sentences from the words in Activity 5 on page 15 of your Class Book.	Talk about the pie chart on page 18.
What happens in *The castle towers?*	Talk about the bar chart on page 18.	Sing the song *Now we've already been on some of the rides …*	Talk about The Eden Project.
Decide what to do at a theme park with a friend.	Say the chant *I'm on the roller coaster, going up and down. …*	Talk about the line graph on page 19.	Do a role play: you are talking about a place you've visited.

3 At the airport

1 Look, listen and repeat. 🔊 1.36

1 arrivals   2 departures   3 get your boarding card   4 check in your luggage
5 go through security   6 security guard   7 show your passport   8 pilot
9 flight attendant   10 board the plane   11 go to your gate   12 passenger

2 Look and write *true* or *false*. 📝

1. You get your boarding card when you board the plane.
2. You check in your luggage when you go through security.
3. The flight attendant meets you when you board the plane.
4. You show your passport after you go through security.
5. You go to your gate after you show your passport.
6. You can see two flight attendants on the plane.
7. A man is walking towards Gate 4.
8. The security guard is wearing a black uniform.

3 Point to the picture. Ask and answer.

What do you do here?
You check in your luggage.
Who's this?
The pilot.

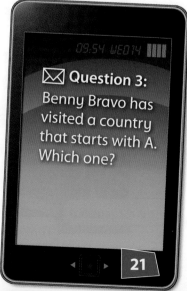

09:54 WED 14

✉ **Question 3:**
Benny Bravo has visited a country that starts with A. Which one?

1 Listen and read. 🎧 1.39

2 Look and say. Which sentences are in the story?

He's been	to Argentina	!
He hasn't been	to Russia	!
Has he	ever	been	to China	?
Yes,	he has	No,	he hasn't	.

I went	to Africa	last month	.
I didn't go	to Mexico	in February	.
When	did he go	to Argentina	?

Tip

• We use the **Present perfect simple** to talk about a finished action, when we don't know the time of the action.

• We use the **Present perfect simple** when the time of the action isn't important.

• We use the **Past simple** when we know the time of the action.

• We use the **Past simple** when the time of the action is important.

Remember: Don't use a past time phrase with the Present perfect:

✗ ~~He's eaten two toffee apples yesterday.~~

3 Look at the pictures and finish the dialogue.

1. Argentina 2006, India 2007, France 2001
2. France 2004, England 2002
3. England 2001, France 2003, Argentina 2005
4. India 2003, England 2006, Argentina 2002
5. India 2004, France 2005, Argentina 2007
6. India 2002, England 2007

Has she ever been to Argentina?

No, she hasn't.

Has she ever been to France?

Yes, she has.

When did she go?

In 2004.

Number 2 ?

Yes!

4 Listen and repeat. 🔘 1.40

Has she ever been to Argentina?

When did she go?

In 2003.

5 Choose a different picture. Make sentences and questions.

Has she	ever	been	to Argentina	to India
to France	to England	?	Yes,	No,
she has	she hasn't	.
When	did she go	?
She went	in 1999	.

6 Complete the grammar table.

Would you like to fly? Read this Greek myth.

1 Read the text quickly. Which of these people and things are in the story?

a an island   b a lion   c the sea   d Theseus, the king's enemy   e a fish

f The Queen of Crete   g Daedalus, a famous inventor   h Icarus, a boy   i the sunboy

DAEDALUS, THE MAN WHO COULD FLY

Daedalus lived on the island of Crete with his <u>son</u> Icarus. He was a famous inventor and <u>craftsman</u>. Daedalus worked for the King of Crete. One day he made the King very angry. He helped one of the King's enemies, Theseus, escape from the island with the King's <u>daughter</u>. The King sent his guards to catch Daedalus. The guards were everywhere. There was no escape from the island.

"We can't hide and we can't use a boat", said Daedalus, "The only way to leave this island is to fly!" So Daedalus made some wings for

himself and his son. He made them with wood and feathers. He glued the feathers to the wood with <u>wax</u>. He gave Icarus his wings. Before they started flying he said to Icarus "Remember, wax <u>melts</u> when it is hot. Don't fly near the sun!"

They jumped off a <u>cliff</u> and started to fly. At first Icarus

followed his father, but then he started to fly higher and higher. His father called him, but he didn't listen. He loved flying and he wanted to fly as high as he could. He flew nearer and nearer the sun and the air got hotter and hotter. Then the wax melted and the feathers fell off the wings. Icarus waved his arms, but he couldn't fly without wings. He fell out of the sky into the sea. The sea is now called the Icarian Sea and the island where he is buried is called Icaria.

2 Find these words in the text.

1 someone who makes beautiful things

2

3

4 candles are made of this

5 changes to a liquid

6

3 Read the text again and answer the questions.

1 Why was Daedalus famous?
2 Who did he work for?
3 What did Theseus do?
4 How did Daedalus and Icarus try to escape from the island?
5 What did Daedalus use to make the wings?
6 Why did Icarus fly higher than his father?
7 What happened to Icarus's wings?
8 Where did he fall?

1 Listen and find the two photos. 🔊 1.46

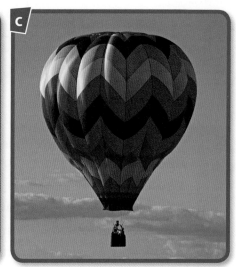

2 Listen again and choose the right answer. 🔊 1.46

1 How does Fred feel when he is in the air?
  a like a bird   **b** like a balloon
  c like Superman

2 Is hang-gliding difficult for Fred?
  a no   **b** yes, at the beginning
  c yes, when it's windy

3 How long can experts stay in the air?
  a 4 hours   **b** 20 hours   **c** 24 hours

4 What's it like in the air?
  a quiet and warm   **b** quiet and cold
  c warm and windy

5 Which bird did he fly with?
  a a parrot   **b** an eagle   **c** a falcon

6 Where is Polly scared?
  a in the air   **b** in the plane
  c on the ground

7 How old was Polly when she started?
  a 40   **b** 16   **c** 14

8 What does she like about being in the air?
  a seeing everything from the air
  b falling fast   **c** floating

9 What did she break?
  a her arm   **b** her leg   **c** her shoulder

3 Listen and find the missing words. 🔊 1.47

Have you ever been ___1___ ?

Yes, I have, ___2___ .

Have you ever hurt yourself?

Yes, once. I broke my ___3___ .

What happened?

I landed ___4___ .

Oh no!

1 parachuting   hang-gliding   in a hot air balloon

2 once   lots of times

3 ankle   arm   finger

4 in the sea   on the road   in a river

4 Do the role play with your partner. Choose different words.

Perspective in art

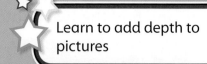

Learn to add depth to pictures

1 Look, listen and repeat. 1.48

2 Listen, read and answer. 1.49

How to add depth to a picture

Perspective

Artists use special techniques to give a feeling of space and distance in their pictures. Look at this finished picture of a runway.

Which plane looks closer?

Which plane looks further away?

This effect is created by drawing in perspective.

Now follow the steps for drawing perspective in a picture.

1 Prepare your picture.
   Draw a horizon line. Draw a dot on the horizon. This is the vanishing point.

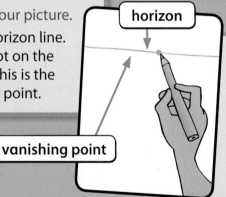

horizon

vanishing point

2 Draw the runway.
   Draw two lines from the bottom of the picture to the vanishing point. These are the sides of the runway. They join at the vanishing point. Then draw some lights along the runway.

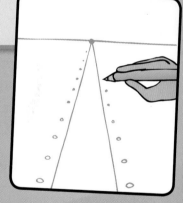

3 Start drawing the airport building.
   Draw a rectangle. This is the front side of the building. Connect three corners of the rectangle to the vanishing point. These are the sight lines.

sight lines

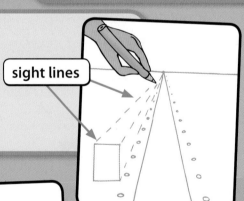

4 Draw the sides of the building.
   Draw a horizontal line and a vertical line between the sight lines. This is the back side of the building. Finish the building by drawing along the sight lines.

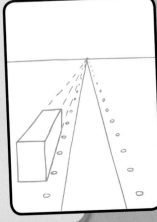

5 Finish the picture.
   Rub out the sight lines. Add details to the building and the runway. Use the techniques in the next section.

Words to describe perspective

Other useful techniques

Size

Which flags look bigger: the ones in the foreground or the ones in the background?

Draw items in the foreground bigger than items in the background.

background

foreground

Lines

Which lines are thicker: the ones in the foreground or the ones in the background?

Use thicker lines to draw items in the foreground. Use thinner lines to draw items in the background.

1 Read the text again and make sentences.

1 The horizon is where	a things look closer.
2 The less important things are usually	b when you draw a picture with perspective.
3 The important things are usually	c look closer to you in a picture.
4 Big things	d in the background of a picture
5 Small things	e look farther away from you in a picture.
6 Thick lines can make	f things look further away.
7 Thin lines can make	g the earth and sky meet.
8 You need a vanishing point and sight lines	h in the foreground of a picture.

2 Listen and say *true* or *false*. 1.50

Talk about it!

3 Talk about the four pictures on this page.

There are some hang-gliders in the background.   planes
foreground

There's a balloon in the foreground.   a boy with a kite
The yellow kite looks closer than the green kite.   further away

Me and my world

1 Read the questions and find the answers.

Which paragraph talks about ...

a kayaking?

b walking?

c New Zealand and New Zealanders?

d the Abel Tasman National Park?

Abel Tasman National Park

NEW ZEALAND

① Hi, my name's Adele and I live in New Zealand. It's a beautiful country with two big islands and lots of small ones. We've got mountains, rivers, lakes and beautiful beaches too. The animals here are really unusual – there are some, like the kiwi bird, that you don't find in any other part of the world. People here often go walking, biking and camping, and there are fourteen National Parks where you can enjoy nature and outdoor activities.

② I've been to lots of National Parks, but my favourite is the Abel Tasman. It's on the north coast of the South Island. It's got sandy beaches with amazing cliffs. I went camping there last year with my family. It was great. We arrived at the campsite in a water taxi on Friday lunchtime. We wanted to have a barbecue, but we couldn't because there was a fire alert. We had to have sandwiches!

③ After lunch, Dad checked with the visitor centre and they said the weather was going to be good, so we went kayaking. It was fantastic, the water was clear and we could see fish swimming in the sea. The best part was when we saw some dolphins swimming around us. My sister and I wanted to dive in with them. But Dad didn't think it was a good idea because it's difficult to get back into the kayak.

④ The next day we trekked along the coast. The path crosses an estuary, so Mum checked the tides. You can only cross two hours before or after high tide, at other times it is dangerous because the water covers the beach. The walk was fun except for one part. We had to cross a river on a suspension bridge. It was 46 metres long and it moved when you walked on it. I was really scared. When we were back at the campsite we watched the stars. I didn't want to go home.

2 Read again and answer the questions.

1 How many big islands is New Zealand made of?
2 Why is the kiwi bird unusual?
3 What can you do in the New Zealand National Parks?
4 Where is the Abel Tasman park?
5 How did they arrive at the park?
6 Why did they have sandwiches for lunch?
7 Where can you ask for a weather report?
8 Who wanted to swim with the dolphins?
9 When is it safe to cross the estuary?
10 Why was she scared?

3 Think about it! Then discuss in groups.

Adele had a lot of fun at the National Park, but the most important thing is that she and her family were safe.

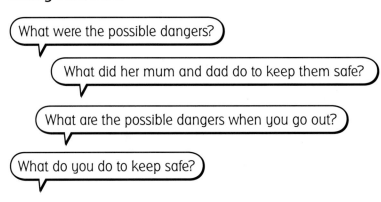

What were the possible dangers?

What did her mum and dad do to keep them safe?

What are the possible dangers when you go out?

What do you do to keep safe?

Learning to learn - Writing a blog

You can write about anything on a blog – yourself, your family, your friends, your hobbies. You can add photos and audio or video recordings too.

1 You could write about the books you've read, your favourite sport, or your pet. You can add to it every week, like a diary.

2 You can look at your friends' blogs and write comments. Remember: be nice!

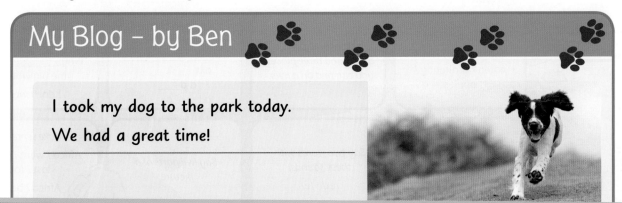

My Blog – by Ben

I took my dog to the park today.
We had a great time!

Revision

Play the game!

How to play
- Play in two teams of two.
- You need six paper counters each. **Team 1**: write *1* on your counters. **Team 2**: write *2* on your counters.
- Put a counter on the board; it must sit on top of another counter if it isn't on the bottom row.
- Follow the instructions.
- The first team to make a line of **four** is the winner.

Make questions.
you / on / Saturdays / do / what / ?
do / now / what / doing / are / ? / you

Say two words with these sounds.
/əʊ/ /ɒ/

Make questions.
some / foreground / there / balloons / are / the / in .

Say these theme park words.
a b_____ w_____
a r_____ c_____
b_____ c_____
a w_____

Say two words with these sounds.
/dʒ/ /tʃ/

What is the boys' least favourite attraction?

Say these words for nature features.
a sm_____ i _____
a st_____ h_____
a d_____ l_____
a h_____ w_____

Make questions.
China / he / ? / been / has / ever / to
did / go / China / when / ? / he / to

Make a sentence.
waterslide. / I / yet / haven't / the / on / been

Complete the questions.
How _____ is it?
_____ 30m long.
How _____ is it?
_____ 10m high.

Say these airport words.
ch_____ in your l_____
g_____ your b_____ c_____
g_____ through s_____
s_____ your p_____

Complete the sentence.
Where's the bridge?
It's on the _____
_____ of the river.

Make sentences.
at / Maths / 9.00 / .
usually / We / have
playing / today / tennis / We're / .

Say these words for nature features.
a d_____ c_____
a l_____ b_____
a w_____ r_____
a n_____ s_____

Complete the conversation.
Hello, _____ I speak to Julia, _____ ?
_____ , she
_____ _____ .

Say four ways you can organize information visually.

Make a sentence.
toffee / He's / two / eaten / . / already / apples

Say the three parts of a river and three places you can find on a river.

Say these theme park words.
a m_____-g_____-r_____
a b_____ c_____
a p_____
a t_____ a_____

Complete the question and answer.
Why _____ _____ go on the big wheel?
_____ , I don't want _____ .

Say these airport words.
d_____ a_____
pa_____ pi_____
f_____ a_____
s_____ g_____

Say two words with these sounds.
/eɪ/ /e/

Say five parts of a picture.

Make sentences.
Africa / went / month / last / to / .
Africa / been / He's / . / to

4 At the weather centre

1 Look, listen and repeat. ⊚ 2.1

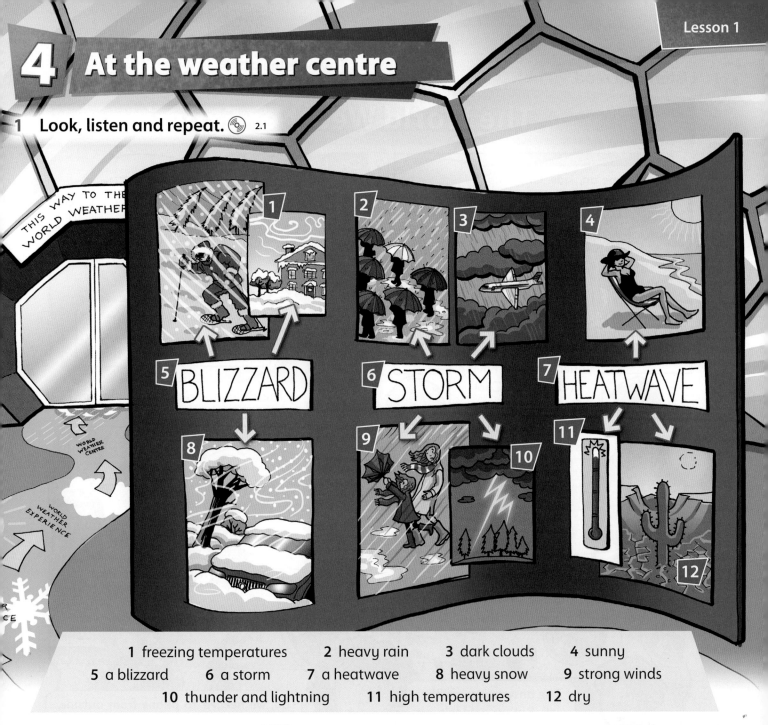

1 freezing temperatures   2 heavy rain   3 dark clouds   4 sunny
5 a blizzard   6 a storm   7 a heatwave   8 heavy snow   9 strong winds
10 thunder and lightning   11 high temperatures   12 dry

2 Look and write *true* or *false*. 📝

1 In a blizzard there is heavy snow.
2 In a storm there are freezing temperatures.
3 In a heatwave there are strong winds.
4 In a storm there is thunder and lightning.
5 In a heatwave there are dark clouds.
6 In a blizzard there is thunder and lightning.
7 In a storm it's sunny.
8 In a heatwave there are very high temperatures.

3 Ask and answer.

What's the weather like in a heatwave?

There are very high temperatures.

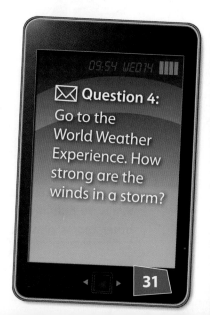

09:54 WED 14

✉ **Question 4:**
Go to the World Weather Experience. How strong are the winds in a storm?

1 Listen and read. 🎧 2.4

The World Weather Experience

2   **Look and say. Which sentences are in the story?**

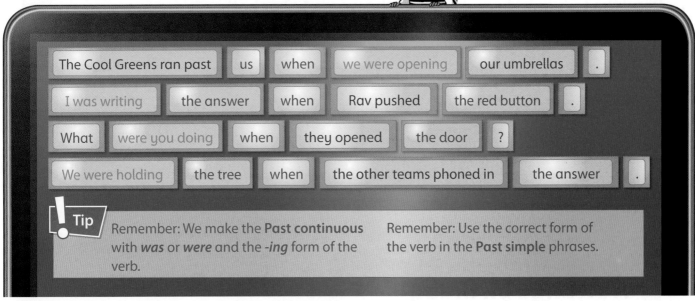

| The Cool Greens ran past | us | when | we were opening | our umbrellas | . |

| I was writing | the answer | when | Rav pushed | the red button | . |

| What | were you doing | when | they opened | the door | ? |

| We were holding | the tree | when | the other teams phoned in | the answer | . |

> **! Tip**
>
> Remember: We make the **Past continuous** with *was* or *were* and the *-ing* form of the verb.
>
> Remember: Use the correct form of the verb in the **Past simple** phrases.

3   **Look at the pictures and finish the dialogue.**

What was he doing when the storm started?

He was playing football.

What was he doing when the storm stopped?

He was watching television.

Number ____ ?

Yes!

4   **Listen and repeat.** 🔘 2.5

What was he doing when the storm started?

He was playing football.

5   **Choose a different picture. Make questions and answers.**

| What | was he doing | when | the storm |

| started | stopped | ? | He was | playing |

| eating | sleeping | watching | football |

| an ice cream | on the computer |

| television | . |

6   **Complete the grammar table.**

Have you ever experienced extreme weather? Read this web page.

1 Read the text quickly and number the words 1, 2 or both.

cow   door   football   thunder   raining   garden   window   bed

http://www.weatherstories.com   Search

a ball lightning

A strange birthday party

By Tiffany, Ontario, Canada

This happened last year at my birthday party. It was cloudy and raining and we could hear thunder too. It was tea time and I was cutting the cake. The windows were open. Suddenly we saw a ball of fire come through the window. It was orange and about the size of a football. The ball of fire began to zigzag around the room, then it climbed up a wall, and finally it disappeared under the door. We were amazed and a bit scared too! I told my teacher and she said it was 'ball lightning'. She told me that ball lightning is very rare.

b tornado

A scary afternoon

By Max, Colorado, USA

One day last summer I was playing with my brother in the garden. Suddenly the sky turned dark. Then the thunder and lightning started and we could see a tornado forming in the clouds. It was very near. We ran into the house and went into the cellar. The tornado went past the house. We felt the house shake and we could hear things flying through the air. I was terrified. When it finished we went outside. We saw my brother's bed in the middle of the garden, and a cow on top of the house! The cow was fine, but a bit surprised. Everybody in the town was alright, but the tornado destroyed a lot of houses.

2 Find these words in the text.

1 very surprised

2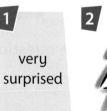

3 in the centre

4

5 very unusual

6 the season when it is hot and dry

7

8

3 Read the text again and answer the questions.

1   When did Tiffany see ball lightning?
2   What was the weather like?
3   What was she doing when the lightning ball came in?
4   What did it look like?
5   How did it go out of the house?
6   How did they feel?
7   When did Max see the tornado?
8   What was he doing?
9   How did the weather change?
10 Where did they hide?
11 How did he feel?
12 What did they see after the tornado?

1 **Listen and find the three photos.** 2.11

2 **Listen again and choose the right answer.** 2.11

1 What can't the reporter see?
a the garden **b** the door
c the windows

2 Which window did the man climb out of?
a bathroom **b** kitchen **c** bedroom

3 How many snowmen have the children made?
a five **b** three **c** six

4 What are the children going to build?
a a snow house **b** a snowdog
c a tunnel

5 Where does the woman go every year?
a to the mountains **b** to the beach
c to the shops

6 Who is the woman going to buy food for?
a her friends **b** her family
c her neighbours

3 **Listen and find the missing words.** 2.12

Have you ever seen ___1___ ?

When did you see it?

Where were you?

Was it ___4___ ?

Yes, I have.

___2___

___3___

___5___

1 a storm   a blizzard   a tornado

2 A long time ago.   Last year.   Two years ago.

3 At home.   On holiday.   In France.

4 dangerous   exciting   scary

5 Yes, it was.   No, it wasn't.

4 **Do the role play with your partner. Choose different words.**

Weather maps

1 **Look, listen and repeat.** 🔊 2.13

2 **Listen, read and answer.** 🔊 2.14

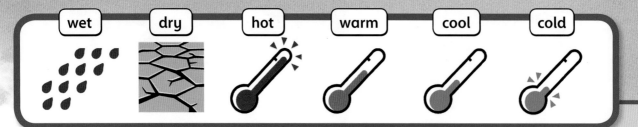

| wet | dry | hot | warm | cool | cold |

Weather maps

Weather maps tell us about temperature, precipitation, wind, and air pressure. These things all contribute to the weather.

Temperature

The sun heats the earth. The sun's rays hit the earth at different angles. This means it is hot at the equator and cold at the poles.

The temperature is shown on weather maps in °C (degrees Centigrade).

Where is it 3°C? Point to a place.

Precipitation

Water moves from earth to sky in the water cycle. When water falls from clouds, it is called precipitation.

Precipitation is rain, snow, sleet or hail, depending on the temperature.

These are the symbols for clouds.

 sunny, no cloud

 clouds with some sunshine

 clouds with rain and sunshine

 clouds with rain

 clouds with snow

 thunder clouds and storms

Where is it snowing? Point to a place.

Air pressure

Air presses all around us. This is called air pressure.

H This is the symbol for an area of high air pressure. High pressure usually means dry weather.

Where is there high pressure?

L This is the symbol for an area of low air pressure. Low pressure usually means cloudy, wet weather.

Where is there low pressure?

Air masses, fronts and wind

Air moves around the earth in big blocks or masses. They can be cold, warm, wet or dry. When a cold air mass and a warm air mass meet, a front forms and the weather changes.

 This is the symbol for a warm front. Warm fronts bring wet weather.

Find a warm front.

 This is the symbol for a cold front. Cold fronts bring cold weather.

Find a cold front.

 Wind is moving air. This is the symbol for wind – the number shows the speed in kilometres per hour (kph) and the arrow shows the direction of the wind.

Where is the wind speed 5 kph? Point to a place.

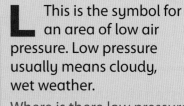

1 Read the text again and make sentences.

1	Weather maps	a	cold weather.
2	Precipitation is	b	in kilometres per hour.
3	We measure temperature	c	cloudy, wet weather.
4	High pressure usually means	d	wet weather.
5	Low pressure usually means	e	in degrees Centigrade.
6	A cold front usually means	f	tell us about the weather.
7	A warm front usually means	g	dry weather.
8	We measure wind speed	h	the water that falls from clouds.

2 Listen and say which picture. 2.15

Talk about it!

3 Talk about the weather map.

What's the weather like here?
It's a nice day to play sport.

There's an area of high pressure.
It's cloudy.
There's a thunderstorm.
The temperature is 5 °C.
The wind speed is 15 kilometres per hour.

It isn't
to go for a walk   to go sailing
low
snowing   rainy   sunny

1 **Complete with the correct form of the verb.**
Listen to the song and check. 2.16

| crash | play | run | start | run | flash | come | play | sit | go |

We **1** a game,
Outside one day,
When all of a sudden
It **2** to rain.

A storm **3** when
We **4** outside,
So we all had to run and hide!

The thunder **5**
When the lightning **6** down,
So we all **7** fast
From the football ground.

We **8** at home
When the storm **9** away,
So we all **10** out
To play again!

2 **Play the game.**

How to play
- Play in two teams of two.
- You need six paper counters each. **Team 1:** write *1* on your counters. **Team 2:** write *2* on your counters.
- Put a counter on the board. You can put it on the bottom row, or above another counter.
- Read and do.
- The first team to make a line of <u>three</u> is the winner.

Talk about the picture on page 31 of your Class Book.	What happened at Tiffany's birthday party?	Make sentences from the words in Activity 5 on page 33 of your Class Book.	What do you know about temperature and about air pressure?
What happens in *The World Weather Experience?*	What do you know about preciptiation and about the wind?	Sing the song *We were playing a game ...*	What happened when Max was playing in the garden?
Talk about the weather in your area today.	Say the chant *In a blizzard, when we're freezing ...*	Talk with a friend about two of the photos on page 37.	Do a role play: imagine you have experienced extreme weather.

5 On the film set

1 Look, listen and repeat. 🔘 2.17

| 1 stuntman | 2 extra | 3 director | 4 camera operator | 5 fan | 6 shake hands |
| 7 bodyguard | 8 actor | 9 wave | 10 sign an autograph | 11 reporter |

2 Look and answer the questions. 📝

1 Who is jumping out of a window?
2 Who is interviewing an actor?
3 Who is waving at the actors?
4 Who is signing an autograph?
5 Who is talking to the camera operator?
6 Who is shaking hands?
7 Who is filming the stuntman?
8 Who is wearing a green dress?

3 Point to the people. Ask and answer.

What's this actor doing?

He's talking to the reporter.

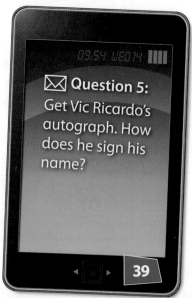

09:54 WED 14

✉ **Question 5:**
Get Vic Ricardo's autograph. How does he sign his name?

1 Listen and read. 🔊 2.20

2 Look and say. Which sentences are in the story?

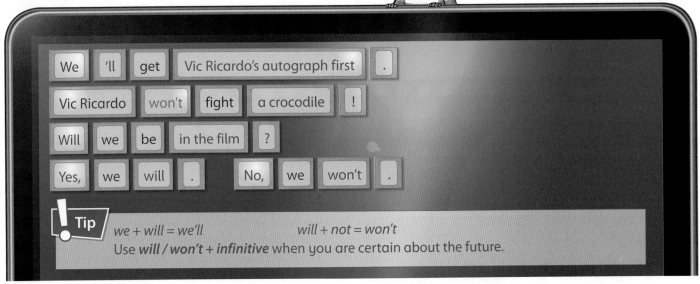

| We | 'll | get | Vic Ricardo's autograph first | . |

| Vic Ricardo | won't | fight | a crocodile | ! |

| Will | we | be | in the film | ? |

| Yes, | we | will | . | No, | we | won't | . |

! **Tip**
we + will = we'll   will + not = won't
Use **will / won't** + infinitive when you are certain about the future.

3 Look at the pictures and finish the dialogue.

	1	2	3	4
June	London	London	Tokyo	Tokyo
July	New York	Buenos Aires	New York	Buenos Aires
August	Tokyo	Tokyo	London	London
September	Buenos Aires	New York	Buenos Aires	New York

Will he be in London in June?

Yes, he will.

Will he be in New York in July?

No, he won't.

It's number ____.

Yes!

4 Listen and repeat. 2.21

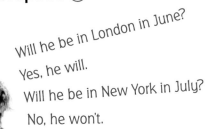

Will he be in London in June?

Yes, he will.

Will he be in New York in July?

No, he won't.

5 Choose a different picture. Make questions and answers.

| Will | he | be | in Tokyo | in London |

| in Buenos Aires | in New York | in June |

| in July | in August | in September | ? |

| Yes, | No, | he | will | won't | . |

6 Complete the grammar table.

will   won't

What's your all-time favourite film? Read these reviews.

1 Guess which words are in each review. Then read quickly and check.

princess   dancing   green   snake   boy   fire   dragon   bear   tiger   secret   donkey   house

Film reviews

★★★★★

Film: Shrek • Reviewed by: Cathy • Age 12

Shrek is my favourite film ever! Shrek is an ogre. He is green and bad-tempered. He lives alone in a swamp. He meets a donkey called Donkey. Donkey is my favourite character! He is really funny. Donkey is always nice to Shrek but Shrek isn't always nice to him. Together, they rescue Princess Fiona. She is a prisoner in a dragon's castle. Fiona is not a normal fairytale princess; she can do karate, she does crazy things, and she has a secret. Shrek has a secret too, he loves Fiona, but he doesn't tell her. He thinks he is too ugly for her. What's Fiona's secret? Do Shrek and Fiona get married? Watch the film and find out!

★★★★★

Film: The Jungle Book • Reviewed by: Chris • Age 11

The Jungle Book is a brilliant film. I've seen it more than twenty times. It is full of funny characters and there are some great songs in it too. The film is set in India and the main character is a boy called Mowgli. He hasn't got a human family. He lives in the jungle with the wolves, and he can talk to animals. The tiger, Shere Khan hates humans and he wants to kill Mowgli. So Mowgli has to go to a village because he isn't safe in the jungle. Mowgli and his friends have lots of adventures on their way. Baloo the bear is my favourite character. He loves eating, singing, dancing and having a good time. The best scene is when the monkeys are dancing with Mowgli. Go and see it, it's a great film!

2 Find these words in the text.

1

2 doesn't like

3 not patient, angry

4 very, very silly

5 the opposite of pretty or beautiful

6

7

3 Read the text again and make sentences.

1	Shrek	a	hasn't got a human family.
2	Donkey	b	can talk to animals.
3	Princess Fiona	c	lives in a swamp.
4	Shrek	d	doesn't tell Fiona his secret.
5	Mowgli	e	can do karate.
6	Shere Khan	f	doesn't like humans.
7	Mowgli	g	is Cathy's favourite character.
8	Baloo	h	is Chris's favourite character.

1 Listen and count. 🎧 2.27

How many questions does Alice answer correctly?　　How many questions does Jack answer correctly?

2 Listen again and choose the right answer. 🎧 2.27

1 When was *Toy Story 3* released?
   a in 2009　　**b** in 2007　　**c** in 2010

2 How many Oscars did *Toy Story 3* win?
   a one　　**b** two　　**c** four

3 What is the name of the cowgirl?
   a Tessie　　**b** Jessie

4 When was *E. T.* released?
   a 1982　　**b** 1992　　**c** 2002

5 How many Oscars did *E. T.* win?
   a one　　**b** two　　**c** four

6 How much did it cost to make *E. T.*?
   a $10.5 million　　**b** $12.5 million
   c $15.5 million

3 Listen and find the missing words. 🎧 2.28

What's your favourite film of all time?

That's ___1___ !
I love ___2___ .

Oh yes, that's a ___3___ film.

Which character do you like best?

___4___

Why?

I think ___5___ really ___6___ .

1 difficult　easy

2 *Shrek*　*The Jungle Book*　*E.T.*

3 great　brilliant　fantastic

4 Donkey.　Fiona.　Baloo.

5 he's　she's

6 brave　nice　kind

4 Do the role play with your partner. Choose different words.

The history of films

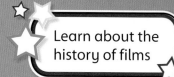

Learn about the history of films

1 Look, listen and repeat. 2.29

| shoot a film | camera | subtitle | frame | projector |

Farewell good friend

2 Listen and read. When were the films made? Look at the timeline. 2.30

How are moving images made?

Films are made of thousands of frames. Each frame has a picture which is a bit different from the one before. When the frames pass quickly before our eyes, the pictures appear to move. This is why they are often called movies.

Early films

Thomas Edison made a camera that could make moving images. He made a five-second film of his assistant sneezing. It is called *Fred Ott's Sneeze*. It was **one of the first films.** You had to watch it through a hole in a box. Only one person could see it at a time.

The Lumière brothers lived in France. They invented a camera with a projector. Now lots of people could see a film together. They made a film called *The Arrival of a Train*. It was **one of the first films to have an audience.** The train looked very real – the audience were terrified!

The Great Train Robbery was **the first film to tell a story.** The director used a new technique. First he shot the film. Then he edited it in a studio. He cut up the film and put it together again to make an exciting story.

Fred Ott's Sneeze — 1894

The Arrival of a Train — 1895

The Great Train Robbery — 1903

1911 — Little Nemo in Slumberland

3 Read the text again and answer the questions.

1 What's another name for a film?
2 How many people could see Edison's films at a time?
3 Why was the Lumière brothers' invention important?
4 Why is *The Great Train Robbery* important in film history?
5 How did early films show dialogues?
6 Was it easy to make colour films?
7 How many frames were there in the first cartoon film?
8 Who made *Snow White and the Seven Dwarfs*?

Film words

1 Listen and say which film. 🔊 2.31

Films and sound

The first films didn't have any sound. There was a piano player in the cinema who added music. The audience read dialogue or explanations of the story from written cards. *The Jazz Singer* was **the first film to have sound and dialogue.**

Cartoons

Little Nemo was a cartoon in a newspaper. **The first animated cartoon,** *Little Nemo in Slumberland,* was made from a *Little Nemo* story. It had 4,000 frames or pictures. It was very short. Each frame was drawn by hand. *Snow White and the Seven Dwarfs* was **the first full-length cartoon film.** It was made by Walt Disney.

Films in colour

Early films were made in black and white. It was difficult and expensive to make films in colour. *The Wizard of Oz* was **one of the first colour films.** It started in black and white and then changed to colour. Everyone was amazed when they saw it.

The Jazz Singer — 1927

Snow White and the Seven Dwarfs — 1937

1939 — The Wizard of Oz

Talk about it!

2 Talk about the films.

When was *Snow White* made?	In 1937.
Why is it important?	It was the first full-length cartoon film.
What does the picture show?	The seven dwarfs.

1 **Complete with the correct form of the verb.**
Listen to the song and check. 2.32

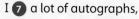

| love | go | sign | give | be | stand | be | shake | keep | be |

I **1** a very famous actor
A real-life movie star.
Tomorrow night is Oscar night.
I **2** there in my car.

I **3** there on the carpet,
I **4** the Press a wave.
My bodyguard **5** there,
And he **6** me safe.

I **7** a lot of autographs,
I **8** hands with my fans.
They **9** me and adore me –
I **10** such a handsome man!

2 **Play the game.**

How to play

- Play in two teams of two.
- You need six paper counters each. **Team 1:** write *1* on your counters. **Team 2:** write *2* on your counters.
- Put a counter on the board. You can put it on the bottom row, or above another counter.
- Read and do.
- The first team to make a line of **three** is the winner.

Talk about the picture on page 39 of your Class Book.	What does Cathy say about the film *Shrek?*	Make sentences from the words in Activity 5 on page 41 of your Class Book.	What do you know about early films?
What happens in *Extras for a day?*	What do you know about films and sound and films in colour?	Sing the song *I'm a very famous actor …*	What does Chris say about *The Jungle Book?*
Describe two people in your Class Book. Talk about their appearance and personality.	Say the chant *I read a fairytale about a bear …*	Talk about when some important films were made.	Talk to a friend about your favourite films.

6 At the concert in the park

1 Look, listen and repeat. 🎧 2.33

1 lights	2 band	3 drummer	4 speakers	5 keyboard player	6 keyboards
7 drums	8 guitarist	9 electric guitar	10 stage	11 lead singer	12 microphone

2 Look and correct the words in blue. 📝

1 There are two men and two women in the band.
2 There are five speakers in the picture.
3 The lead singer is standing on the speakers.
4 The guitarist is playing a blue electric guitar.
5 The drummer has got long hair.
6 The biggest drum is green.
7 There are two keyboards.
8 The keyboard player is holding a microphone.

3 Ask and answer.

Have you ever played an electric guitar?

Yes, I have.

How many drummers are there?

There's one drummer.

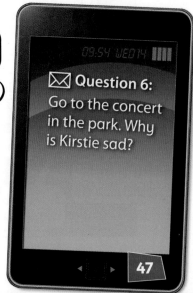

09:54 WED 14

✉ **Question 6:** Go to the concert in the park. Why is Kirstie sad?

Concert words

Lesson 2 ➤ AB page 51

47

1 Listen and read. 🔘 2.36

2 **Look and say. Which sentences are in the story?**

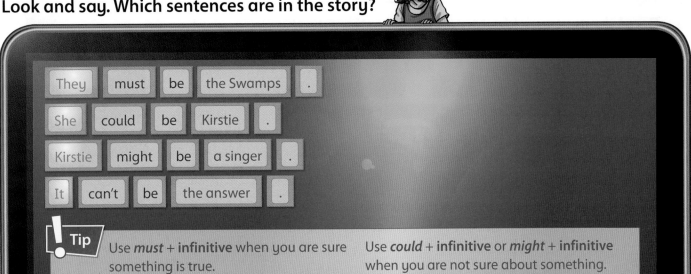

| They | must | be | the Swamps | . |

| She | could | be | Kirstie | . |

| Kirstie | might | be | a singer | . |

| It | can't | be | the answer | . |

! **Tip**
Use *must* + infinitive when you are sure something is true.
Use *can't* + infinitive when you are sure something is not true.

Use *could* + infinitive or *might* + infinitive when you are not sure about something.

3 **Look at the pictures and finish the dialogue.**

Amy   Kay   Jen

I'm thinking of a girl with black trousers. What's her name?

It can't be _____.

It could be Amy. It could be _____. Is it Amy?

Sorry! I'm thinking of Kay.

I'm thinking of a girl with brown hair. What's her name?

It can't be Jen. It can't be _____. It must be _____.

Yes, that's right. It's Amy.

4 **Listen and repeat.** 2.37

It can't be Amy.
It could be Kay.
It must be Jen.

5 **Make more questions and answers about the girls.**

| I'm thinking of a girl with | black trousers |

| a hat | a guitar | drums | brown hair |

| a green T-shirt | blonde hair | a red T-shirt | . |

| What's her name | ? | It | could | can't |

| must | be | Amy | Jen | Kay | . |

6 **Complete the grammar table.**

Stomp is an amazing show. Read this magazine interview.

1 Read the text quickly. Match the questions to the paragraphs.

a How did *Stomp* start?   b Does the audience like *Stomp*?

c Who are the performers?   d What is *Stomp*?

STOMP!

Jessica Taylor talks to the creators of *Stomp*.

Stomp is a theatre show with a difference. There isn't any talking and there isn't any singing, but there is lots of music and dancing. I talked to Luke Cresswell and Steve McNicholas, the creators of *Stomp*.

1 _____

Steve: *Stomp* is all about rhythm. Listen carefully and you can hear rhythm everywhere, on buses, in the supermarket, and tapping on the computer. We use this idea in the show. We make music out of ordinary objects, junk you find at home. We play on things like <u>brooms</u>, matchboxes and <u>pipes</u>. Then we add movement to the music. And because there isn't any language, people all round the world enjoy the show.

2 _____

Luke: Sometimes the performers start as <u>musicians</u>, and sometimes they start as dancers, but in the end they are both

and more! All our performers are very creative and have strong personalities. Everyone who works in *Stomp* adds something new to the show. Sometimes we invite people in the <u>audience</u> to come on stage and join in. Everyone can make rhythm with their hands and bodies and everyone can drum.

3 _____

Steve: We started out as two <u>buskers</u>. Then we did a theatre show in Scotland. Then we travelled round the world with *Stomp*. Sometimes we go to schools and do <u>workshops</u> with the children. We've been on television lots of time too!

3 _____

Luke: They love it! Making music from <u>junk</u> is a new idea, it's really simple and it works very well. When they leave, they use the things around them to make music – the chairs, the doors, their umbrellas. They take the idea of *Stomp* out of the theatre with them.

2 Find these words in the text.

1 people who play music

2

3

4 practical classes

5 people who perform on the street

6 the people who watch a performance

7

3 Read the text again. Correct the false sentences.

1 The performers don't talk or sing in *Stomp*.

2 They use drums and tambourines to make music.

3 When you go to *Stomp* you have to understand English.

4 The performers in *Stomp* add new ideas to the show.

5 Everybody can make rhythms.

6 *Stomp* has travelled around the world.

7 *Stomp* is a television programme.

8 People take some *Stomp* instruments out of the theatre with them.

Reading: An interview

1 Listen and say which things they talk about. 2.43

| brooms | cups | cans | matchboxes | dustbins | hammers | pipes |

2 Listen again and choose the right answer. 2.43

1 When did Rosie go to the show?
   a last week   b yesterday
   c on her birthday

2 What are the dustbins like?
   a noisy   b difficult to play   c exciting

3 How many men and women are there in the show?
   a 8 men and 5 women   b 3 men and 5 women   c 5 men and 3 women

4 What did Adam think of the brooms music?
   a He hated it.   b He liked it.
   c He liked it a lot.

5 What was easy for Rosie?
   a clapping a rhythm
   b playing matchboxes   c dancing

6 What do the children decide to do?
   a make music   b watch the DVD together
   c go to the show together

3 Listen and find the missing words. 2.44

Have you ever been to the theatre?

When did you go?

What did you see?

Yes, I have.

1

I saw 2 .

Was it good?

3

What did you like best?

4

1 Last Christmas.   Last summer.   Last year.

2 a play   a ballet   a puppet show   a musical

3 Yes, I loved it.   No, it was boring.   It was OK.

4 The songs.   The dancing.   The jokes.   The costumes.

4 Do the role play with your partner. Choose different words.

Jazz

1 Look, listen and repeat. 2.45

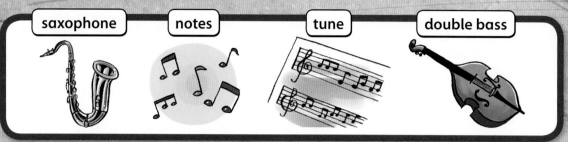

| saxophone | notes | tune | double bass |

2 Listen, read and answer. 2.46

What is jazz?

Jazz developed in the USA at the beginning of the 20th century. Before jazz, the notes of a piece of music were always the same.

Listen. Do you know this tune?

Jazz was a new style of music and musicians started to play very differently. In jazz, the musicians improvise: they take a piece of music and play it in their own style, and add new notes or rhythms. So the same tune played by different jazz musicians always sounds different.

Listen to these jazz tunes. Which do you prefer?

The history of jazz

In the 1700s and 1800s, West Africans were taken to America to work as slaves. Their music was very important to them. They sang when they worked. They used their music and songs to communicate and to express their feelings and their desire to be free. This music is the roots of jazz.

Then, in the 1800s, people from all over the world went to North America to start a new life. Many different nationalities lived in New Orleans. They all had their own kinds of music. African-American and European musicians played together and

You can play jazz on any instrument and there are jazz singers too. Typical instruments are the saxophone, trumpet, piano, drums and double bass.

Jazz musicians make the music personal. They express their own emotions and personality when they play. Listen to these pieces of jazz. How does the music sound: sad, happy or relaxed?

learned from each other. They mixed their different kinds of music, and jazz was born. Rock and roll, hip hop and other kinds of popular music developed from jazz.

3 Read the text again and answer the questions.

1 Where did jazz develop?
2 When did jazz develop?
3 What does *improvise* mean?
4 What are typical jazz instruments?
5 How do jazz musicians make a piece of music personal?
6 Whose music formed the roots of jazz?
7 In which American city did jazz develop?
8 What kinds of music developed from jazz?

1 Listen and say which photo. (◎) 2.47

Talk about it!

2 Listen and talk about the jazz music. (◎) 2.48

I think I can hear a trumpet.   saxophone   clarinet
She's singing.
It sounds like some drums and a double bass.

I like it.   I quite like it.   I don't like it.

It makes me feel happy.   sad   relaxed   sleepy

Me and my world

1 Guess which words are in the text. Read and check.

1 prize	**2** festival	**3** peace	**4** church	**5** flags	**6** competitions
7 strong legs	**8** singing	**9** friend	**10** colourful		

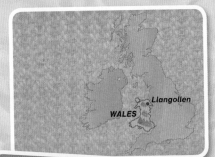

My name's Morgan and I live in Llangollen, a small town in the North of Wales. Our town is famous because we have an international music festival here every year. In our language, Welsh, it's called the Eisteddfod. It started in 1946, just after the end of the Second World War. A man called Harold Tudor heard his milkman singing one morning and it gave him an idea. He decided to start a music festival where people from all over the world could sing, dance and make music together in peace. The first Eisteddfod took place in 1947 with people from more than 14 countries taking part.

After that it got bigger and bigger, and now people come from the four corners of the world. Now there are around 5,000 singers and dancers, and 50,000 visitors. There are shows and competitions, but the most important thing is that everybody shares their culture and learns about other people. The festival is so important that in 2004 it was nominated for the Nobel Peace Prize. We didn't win, but we may get the prize another year.

I always go to the festival. Last year I went to a street dance workshop. It was good fun but very tiring – you need very strong legs! There were lots of people there and not everybody spoke English, but it didn't matter. We laughed a lot, and I made a friend from Japan and another from Greece. After the workshop we all left a message on the Tree of Peace. I wrote 'Let's be friends.' Then we went to watch the Parade of Nations. It's really colourful, everybody wears their national costumes and there is a huge parade through the town, with singing and dancing. In the evening we went to the Children's Storytelling competition. My favourite was an Irish story about some children who were turned into swans. It was a bit sad, but I liked it.

2 Read again and answer the questions.

1. Why is Llangollen famous?
2. What gave Harold Tudor the idea for the festival?
3. When did the first Eisteddfod take place?
4. Where do the people in the festival come from?
5. What happened in 2004?
6. What kind of workshop did Morgan go to?
7. Was it important to speak English at the workshop?
8. Who did she make friends with?
9. What happens at the Parade of Nations?
10. What was the Irish story about?

3 Think about it! Then discuss in groups.

The aim of the Llangollen Eisteddfod is to work for peace in the world.

Can you find four examples of this aim in the text?

How do you learn about people from other cultures?

Learning to learn - Writing to an e-pal

Children all around the world are learning English. You can write to them and find out about them, and practise your English at the same time. But remember! Always check with your parents or your teacher before you contact a person you don't know.

There are sites with lists of children who want e-pals. You can write about yourself, and send photos too!

What would you write in your first e-mail?

Hi! I'm Morgan, I'm your new e-pal. I live in Wales and I speak English and Welsh. I've got two brothers. I love horses! Here's a picture of my horse, Rocky. Do you like riding? Please write soon and tell me about yourself.

Morgan

Revision — Play the game!

How to play
- Play in two teams of two.
- You need six paper counters each. **Team 1**: write *1* on your counters. **Team 2**: write *2* on your counters.
- Put a counter on the board; it must sit on top of another counter if it isn't on the bottom row.
- Follow the instructions.
- The first team to make a line of **four** is the winner.

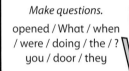

Make questions.
opened / What / when / were / doing / the / ? you / door / they

Say two words with these sounds.
/eə/ /ɑː/

Complete the sentence.
It _____ _____ a double bass and drums.

Say these film set words.
a s_____ a r_____
a b_____ an a_____
a c_____ o_____

Say two words with these sounds.
/ɪ/ /aɪ/

When was Snow White made?

Say these extreme weather words.
a b_____
h_____ s_____
s_____ w_____
f_____ t_____

Make sentences.
. / might / a / Kirstie / singer / be
be / It / . / answer / can't / the

Make a question and answer.
in / ? / we / film / be / a / Will / won't / we / No, / .

Complete the sentences.
It's _____ colder.
I think there's _____ _____ _____ a blizzard.

Say these concert words.
a b_____ a d_____
the l_____ s_____
a g_____ a k_____ p_____

Complete the question and answer.
_____ the weather _____ there?
_____ a thunderstorm.

Make a sentence.
writing / I / button / the / . / when / pushed / was / the / Rav / answer

Say these extreme weather words.
h_____ t_____
t_____ and l_____
d_____ a s_____
h_____ r_____

Complete the sentences.
She _____ _____ three albums.
She _____ _____ two number ones.

Say four words related to films and film making.

Make a sentence.
crocodile / Vic Ricardo / . / fight / won't / a

Say four words to describe the temperature.

Say these film set words.
an e_____ a d_____
s_____ h_____
s_____ an a_____
w_____

Complete the question and answer.
What's he _____ ?
He's _____ and he's _____ moustache.

Say these concert words.
an e_____ g_____
k_____ st_____
l_____ sp_____
m_____

Say two words with these sounds.
/z/ /s/

Say four words related to music and jazz.

Make sentences.
be / the / . / must / Swamps / They
could / She / Kirstie / be / .

7 At the survival camp

1 Look, listen and repeat. 3.1

1 rope	2 fishing line	3 binoculars	4 shelter	5 needle and thread
6 whistle	7 rucksack	8 plasters	9 matches	10 frying pan	11 knife

2 Look and make sentences.

1 We can use the knife
2 We can use the frying pan
3 We can use the whistle
4 We can use the rope
5 We can use the matches
6 We can use the fishing line
7 We can use the needle and thread
8 We can use the rucksack

a to start a fire.
b to carry things.
c to mend clothes.
d to cut things.
e to climb trees.
f to make a loud noise.
g to catch fish.
h to cook food.

3 Ask and answer.

What can we use the knife for?

To cut things.

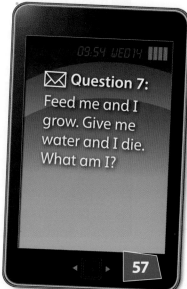

09:54 WED 14

✉ Question 7:
Feed me and I grow. Give me water and I die. What am I?

1 Listen and read. 3.4

The desert island

2 Look and say. Which sentences are in the story?

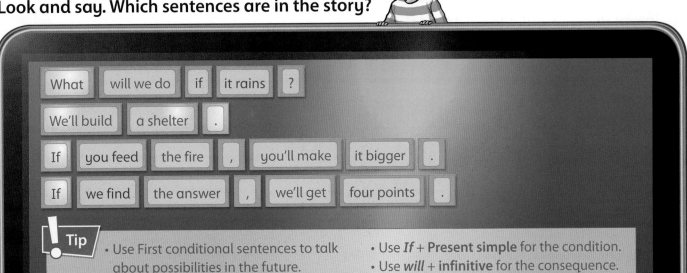

| What | will we do | if | it rains | ? |

| We'll build | a shelter | . |

| If | you feed | the fire | , | you'll make | it bigger | . |

| If | we find | the answer | , | we'll get | four points | . |

!Tip
- Use First conditional sentences to talk about possibilities in the future.
- Use *If* + **Present simple** for the condition.
- Use *will* + **infinitive** for the consequence.

Remember: We use the Present simple but we aren't talking about the present.

3 Look at the pictures and finish the dialogue.

What will he do if he's hungry?

He'll eat coconuts.

What will he do if he sees a snake?

He'll jump in the sea.

Number ___ ?

4 Listen and repeat. 3.5

What will he do if he's hungry?

He'll eat coconuts.

What will he do if he sees a snake?

He'll jump in the sea.

5 Choose a different picture.
Make sentences and questions.

| What | will he do | if | he's | he sees |

| hungry | a snake | ? | He'll climb |

| He'll jump | He'll eat | coconuts |

| insects | a tree | into the sea | . |

6 Complete the grammar table.

I watch *Desert Island Survival* every week. Do the survival quiz!

1 Read the text quickly and find the questions.

1 Which questions ask about food and drink?

2 Which question asks about a place to live?

3 Which question asks about making a fire?

4 Which questions ask about safety?

Desert Island Survival

Have you seen the television show where people have to live on a desert island for three months?

Could you live on a desert island? Do the quiz and find out!

1 If you have to build a hut, which is the best place?

 a) under a tree

 b) on the beach

 c) in a dry, <u>flat</u> area

2 If you need water or other liquids, what **shouldn't** you drink?

 a) coconut milk

 b) sea water

 c) river water

3 If you need some food, which is the safest food to eat?

 a) mushrooms

 b) worms

 c) hairy or brightly-coloured insects

4 Some insects are safe to eat. If you eat them, you will get …

 a) lots of vitamins.

 b) lots of protein.

 c) lots of fat.

5 There are lots of fish in the sea. What is the best time to go fishing?

 a) at <u>midday</u>

 b) at <u>midnight</u>

 c) early in the morning and late in the afternoon

6 Too much sun is bad for you. What **shouldn't** you do?

 a) stay in the <u>shade</u>, and cover yourself

 b) stay in the sea

 c) drink lots of water

7 If you see a snake, what should you do?

 a) pick it up and move it somewhere safe

 b) shout loudly

 c) move away slowly and don't disturb it

8 If you haven't got any matches, how can you make a fire?

 a) use <u>fireflies</u>

 b) put some wood in the sun

 c) use a mirror to focus the sun's rays onto dry wood

Key

1c 2b 3b 4b 5c 6b 7c 8c

Are you a survivor?

7–8 correct answers
Well done. You have got a lot of good ideas. You will be a good companion on a desert island!

3–6 correct answers
OK. You have got some good ideas. But remember to think carefully before you act!

0–2 correct answers
Not very good. Put a survival book in your bag when you travel!

2 Find these words in the text.

1
twelve o'clock in the daytime

2

3

4

5
twelve o'clock at night

6

3 Do the quiz for yourself and then read the key. Answer the questions.

1 What does the answer key say about you?

2 Do you agree?

3 Would you like to live on a desert island?

1 Listen and point to the photos. 🔊 3.11

2 Listen again and choose the right answer. 🔊 3.11

Dialogue 1

1 Why didn't the girl watch *Castaway*?

  a She had to do guitar practice.
  b She doesn't like it.
  c She had to do her homework.

2 What do they use the new hut for?

  a cooking   **b** sleeping   **c** working

3 What was in the hut?

  a some insects   **b** a snake   **c** a spider

4 How did they make a fire?

  a with matches   **b** with a mirror
  c with a stone

Dialogue 2

5 Why didn't the boy watch *Castaway*?

  a He had to help his mother.
  b He had to go to bed.   **c** He had football club.

6 Which activity was difficult for the people?

  a climbing the coconut tree   **b** catching fish
  c making a fire

7 What did they catch?

  a a small octopus   **b** three small fish
  c three big fish

8 What did they have for supper?

  a fish and insects   **b** fish and coconuts
  c insects and coconuts

3 Listen and find the missing words. 🔊 3.12

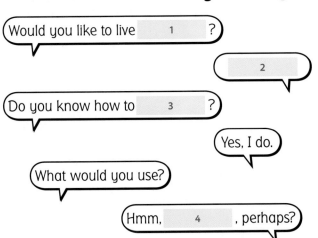

Would you like to live ___1___ ?

___2___

Do you know how to ___3___ ?

Yes, I do.

What would you use?

Hmm, ___4___ , perhaps?

1   in the jungle   in the Antarctic   on a desert island

2   Yes, I think so.   No, no way!   Yes, I'd love it!

3   catch fish   build a hut   make a fire

4   branches   matches   blocks of ice   my hands   string and a paper clip

4 Do the role play with your partner. Choose different words.

Survival features

1 Look, listen and repeat. 3.13

fur	claws	skin	tongue	webbed feet	beak

2 Listen and read. 3.14

There are many different environments on the planet. For example, the poles are very cold, some deserts are hot and dry, and rainforests are warm and wet. It is difficult for humans to survive in extreme environments, but we find animals and plants everywhere.

All animals have to find food, protect themselves and move around. Animals survive because they slowly adapt to the place where they live. There are eight different kinds of bear in the world. They live in different places. They look different and have different habits.

Polar bears live in the Arctic. It is very cold and there is snow on the ground for most of the year. They are carnivores. They hunt and eat fish, seals and sea birds.

Sun bears live in tropical forests in Asia. The forests are hot and wet. Sun bears are omnivores. They eat insects, small animals, fruit and leaves. They spend a lot of time in trees.

Polar bears

The skin under their fur is black. It absorbs the heat from the sun and helps to keep the bears warm.

They have lots of fat under their skin. It keeps them warm.

They have big claws. They are good for catching and killing animals.

Their fur looks white and it is difficult to see them in the snow. It is good camouflage.

They have thick fur. It keeps them warm.

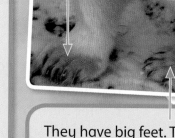

They have big feet. Their feet help them to swim fast and to walk easily on snow.

Sun bears

They have got a very long tongue. They use it to take insects from holes.

They are small so they can climb trees easily.

They have got thick fur. It protects them against the rain and branches, or if they fall out of trees.

They have got big claws and they haven't got any fur on the bottom of their feet. This makes moving in trees easier.

Their dark fur is good camouflage in trees.

1 Read the text again and make sentences.

1	Animals in different environments	a	when they hunt.
2	Polar bears	b	when they climb trees.
3	Sun bears	c	need different kinds of bodies.
4	Polar bears' feet are good for	d	swimming and walking on snow.
5	Polar bears use their claws	e	living in a snowy environment.
6	Sun bears use their claws	f	with their tongues.
7	Polar bears' fur is good for	g	live in a hot, wet environment.
8	Sun bears catch insects	h	live in a cold environment.

2 Listen and say which bird. 🔊 3.15

snowy owl

penguin

golden eagle

humming bird

🗨 Talk about it!

3 Talk about the bears and the birds.

It needs strong claws to hunt with.
It must swim well, because it's got webbed feet.

Its white feathers are good camouflage.
I think it might be nocturnal because it's got big eyes.

a strong beak
fly well   run fast
big wings   strong legs
bright   fur   is
live in trees   eat meat
strong claws   big teeth

1 **Complete with the correct form of the verb.**
Listen to the song and check. 🎵 3.16

| run | see | make | be | see | be | go | be |

We're going to an island,
It's an island in the sun.
We're going to live there for
two weeks.
We think it will be fun.

What will we do if we **1** hungry?
What will we do at night?
What will we do if we **2** a snake?
What will we do for light?

If we **3** hungry, we **4** fishing,
If we **5** a snake, we **6** .
If it **7** cold at night, we **8** a fire,
Don't worry, we'll have fun.

2 **Play the game.**

How to play

- Play in two teams of two.
- You need six paper counters each. **Team 1:** write *1* on your counters. **Team 2:** write *2* on your counters.
- Put a counter on the board. You can put it on the bottom row, or above another counter.
- Read and do.
- The first team to make a line of **three** is the winner.

Talk about the picture on page 57 of your Class Book.	Can you remember four desert island survival tips?	Make sentences from the words in Activity 5 on page 59 of your Class Book.	What do you know about polar bears' survival features?
What happens in *The desert island?*	What do you know about sun bears' survival features?	Sing the song *We're going to an island …*	Describe things that are good to eat and drink on a desert island.
Do a role play: your friend has lost something.	Say the chant *I was fishing in the shade …*	Talk about the survival features of the birds on page 63.	Talk to a friend about living in an extreme environment.

8 | At the planetarium

1 Look, listen and repeat. 🎧 3.17

1 star	2 meteorite	3 satellite	4 space station	5 moon	6 crater
7 Earth	8 alien	9 astronaut	10 space shuttle	11 rocket	12 telescope

2 Look and correct the words in blue.

1 The Earth has got two moons.
2 There are four astronauts in the space shuttle.
3 A boy is looking through a telescope.
4 There are lots of telescopes on the Moon.
5 A meteorite is going to crash into the Earth.
6 A space station is going around the moon.
7 The satellite is flying around Mars.
8 There is a satellite next to the telescope.

3 Ask and answer.

Have you ever seen a satellite?

No, I haven't.

09:54 WED 14

✉ **Question 8:**
How many moons has Mars got?

65

1   Listen and read. 3.20

2 Look and say. Which sentences are in the story?

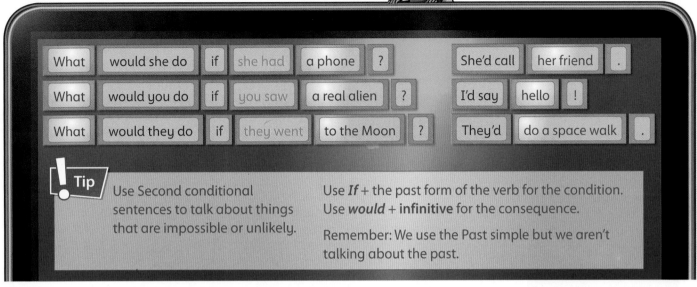

What	would she do	if	she had	a phone	?		She'd call	her friend	.
What	would you do	if	you saw	a real alien	?		I'd say	hello	!
What	would they do	if	they went	to the Moon	?		They'd	do a space walk	.

> **Tip**
> Use Second conditional sentences to talk about things that are impossible or unlikely.
>
> Use *If* + the past form of the verb for the condition. Use *would* + infinitive for the consequence.
>
> Remember: We use the Past simple but we aren't talking about the past.

3 Look at the pictures and finish the dialogue.

4 Listen and repeat. 3.21

What would she do if she saw an alien?
She'd run away.
What would she do if she had a rocket?
She'd go to Mars.

5 Choose a different girl. Make questions and answers.

What	would she do	if	she saw	she had
an alien	a rocket	?	She'd go	
She'd say hello	She'd run away	to the Moon	
to Mars	to Saturn	.	

6 Complete the grammar table.

Can you imagine a holiday in space? Read this brochure from 2060 for some ideas!

1 Read the text quickly. Where are the space tourists on these days?

Day 1   Day 5   Day 7

Welcome to Space Tour!

Visit space with us! It's an experience that's out of this world! This is the programme for a one-week space holiday.

Days 1 and 2

Your <u>amazing</u> holiday starts at SpacePort in New Mexico. When you arrive we prepare you for your trip into space. We show you how to live with no <u>gravity</u>. Just imagine it! You float, your drink floats out of its glass, your money floats out of your pockets and your hair floats away from your head!

Day 3

You <u>board</u> the SpaceJet at nine o'clock in the morning. First we take you high into the sky, to the <u>edge</u> of the atmosphere. Then ninety seconds later you are in space! Now it's only a short journey to SpacePod, our five-star space hotel. You arrive in time for lunch.

Days 4 to 6

Now you've got three days to experience life in space.

- Enjoy looking at space from our <u>huge</u> windows – you can see for 1,500 kilometres. Our space guides help you identify stars and comets.

- Take a space walk! There are two space walks every day. Don't forget your camera!

- Go to the water room for a new experience! It's full of floating balls of water. You can hit them, chase them and have water fights with your friends.

- Use our low-gravity sports room! Imagine playing space football! The ball goes up and you can fly after it! Or would you like to be a gymnast? You can turn triple somersaults and one-handed cartwheels easily when there is no gravity!

Day 7

It's time to go. You get back into the SpaceJet and soon you <u>land</u> on Earth. You've only spent seven days away, but you have had the experience of a lifetime.

2 Find these words in the text.

1
very good

2
the force that makes objects fall down

3
the furthest limit

4
get onto a plane or a train

5
very, very big

6
when a plane leaves the air and touches the ground

3 Read the text again and answer the questions.

1 How long is the trip?
2 Where does the trip start?
3 What happens when there is no gravity?
4 What is your first meal at the space hotel?
5 How far can you see out of the window?
6 How many space walks are there every day?
7 Where can you play with water?
8 What can you do in the low-gravity sports room?

1 Listen and say which things are mentioned. 🔘 3.27

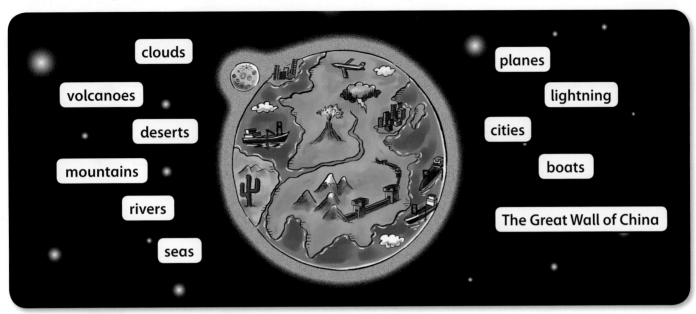

clouds

volcanoes

deserts

mountains

rivers

seas

planes

lightning

cities

boats

The Great Wall of China

2 Listen again and choose the right answer. 🔘 3.27

1 How many times has Arnie been to space?
  a two
  b four
  c six

2 What does he like best?
  a flying the spaceship
  b playing in the water room
  c looking at Earth

3 What colour is Earth from space?
  a white
  b blue
  c green

4 What's the most amazing thing he has seen?
  a a volcano erupting
  b a storm with lightning
  c the desert

5 What can you see that is made by humans?
  a The London Eye
  b The Great Wall of China
  c The Pyramids

6 Why hasn't he seen his home town?
  a It's too small.
  b It's in the mountains.
  c It's in Australia.

3 Listen and find the missing words. 🔘 3.28

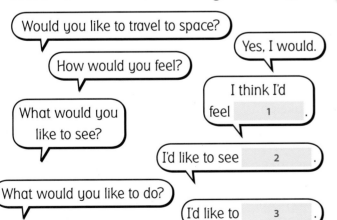

Would you like to travel to space?

Yes, I would.

How would you feel?

I think I'd feel   1   .

What would you like to see?

I'd like to see   2   .

What would you like to do?

I'd like to   3   .

1 a bit scared   very excited   fine

2 The Great Wall of China   a volcano   the desert

3 go on a space walk   play low-gravity football   do gymnastics

4 Do the role play with your partner. Choose different words.

The solar system

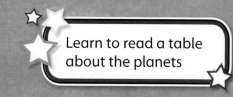

1 **Look, listen and repeat.** 🔊 3.29

2 **Listen and read.** 🔊 3.30

The solar system

There are billions of stars in space. They are balls of gas that produce heat and light. The Sun is the nearest star to Earth. It is the centre of the solar system. Eight planets go around the Sun. They are Mercury, Venus, Earth, Mars, Jupiter, Saturn, Uranus and Neptune.

Moons

Some planets have got moons. A moon is a satellite that travels around a planet. Earth has got one moon. Jupiter has got sixty-three!

Distance from the Sun

Mercury is nearest the Sun. Neptune is furthest away from the Sun. Earth is the third planet from the Sun; it is 150 million kilometres away. It would take a space rocket seven months to travel to the Sun from the Earth.

diameter

Size

The planets have different diameters. Mercury is the smallest, and Jupiter is the biggest. Jupiter's diameter is eleven times bigger than Earth's.

Length of a day

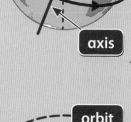
axis

Planets turn on their axis. A day is the time it takes a planet to turn once. Earth turns once in 24 hours so one Earth day is 24 hours long. Some planets, like Saturn, turn very fast and have short days. A day on Saturn is the same as 10 hours and 14 minutes on Earth. Other planets, like Venus, turn slowly and have long days. A day on Venus is the same as 243 days on Earth!

Length of a year

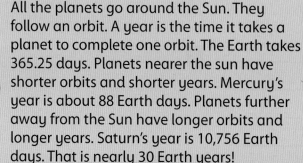
orbit

All the planets go around the Sun. They follow an orbit. A year is the time it takes a planet to complete one orbit. The Earth takes 365.25 days. Planets nearer the sun have shorter orbits and shorter years. Mercury's year is about 88 Earth days. Planets further away from the Sun have longer orbits and longer years. Saturn's year is 10,756 Earth days. That is nearly 30 Earth years!

Mercury

Venus

Earth

Mars

Jupiter

Saturn
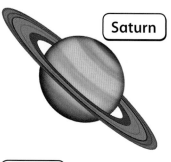

Uranus
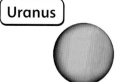

Neptune

1 **Read the text again and answer the questions.**

1 What is in the centre of the solar system?

2 How many planets are there in the solar system?

3 Do all planets have moons?

4 How far is the Earth from the Sun?

5 Which is the smallest planet?

6 Is a day the same length on all planets?

7 Are all orbits the same length?

8 Why does Mercury have a short year?

2 **Listen and say which planet.** 🔊 3.31

Information about the planets Note: all times are Earth times.				
Planet	**A day**	**A year**	**Number of moons / satellites**	**Travelling time from Earth in a space rocket**
Mercury	59 days	2 months 4 weeks	0	5 months 2 weeks
Venus	243 days	7 months 2 weeks	0	3 months 2 weeks
Earth	24 hours	12 months 6 hours	1	–
Mars	24 hours 37 minutes	2 years 11 months	2	5 months 1 week
Jupiter	10 hours 40 minutes	11 years 9 months	63	1 year 6 months
Saturn	10 hours 14 minutes	29 years 5 months	56	2 years 5 months 2 weeks
Uranus	17 hours 12 minutes	84 years 1 month	27	8 years 6 months
Neptune	16 hours 7 minutes	164 years 9 months	13	12 years

Talk about it!

3 **Talk about the planets.**

What colour is Mars?

How long is a day on Mars?

How long is a year on Mars?

How many moons has Mars got?

How long would it take to travel to Mars?

1 **Complete with the correct form of the verb.**
Listen to the song and check. 3.32

| watch out | have | go | study | watch | fly | have | be | visit | fly | travel |

If I **1** a telescope, I'd watch the sky at night.
I **2** craters on the moon
I **3** for moving lights.

If I **4** an astronaut, I **5** around the Sun.
I **6** Mars and Jupiter.
I'd orbit the Earth for fun.

If I **7** a rocket, I'd travel all the way to the stars!
I **8** right through the universe, I'd have a big house on Mars!

If I **9** to Saturn, I **10** around its rings.
I **11** for large meteorites.
I'd see fantastic things.

2 **Play the game.**

How to play

- Play in two teams of two.
- You need six paper counters each. **Team 1:** write *1* on your counters. **Team 2:** write *2* on your counters.
- Put a counter on the board. You can put it on the bottom row, or above another counter.
- Read and do.
- The first team to make a line of <u>three</u> is the winner.

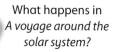

Talk about the picture on page 65 of your Class Book.	What can you remember about Day 1 and Day 3 of the Space Tour?	Make sentences from the words in Activity 5 on page 67 of your Class Book.	What do you know about the length of a day on a planet?
What happens in *A voyage around the solar system?*	What do you know about the length of a year on a planet?	Sing the song *If I had a telescope, ...*	What can you remember about Day 7 of the Space Tour?
What could this be? Why?	Say the chant *It's great here at SpacePort ...*	What can you remember about Days 4 to 6 of the Space Tour?	Talk to your partner about space travel.

9 At the museum

1 Look, listen and repeat. 🔊 3.33

1 first floor	2 display	3 lift	4 entrance	5 ticket office	6 lockers	7 stairs
8 ground floor	9 exit	10 information desk	11 headphones	12 audio guide		

2 Look and correct the words in blue.

1 There's a girl looking at a display of masks.
2 There are two men sitting at the information desk.
3 There are some red headphones.
4 There's a man putting a rucksack into a locker.
5 There's a man giving out the audio guides.
6 There's a man and a woman going down the stairs.
7 There are two people standing in the lift.
8 There's a security guard standing next to the exit.

3 Point to the picture. Ask and answer.

What's the girl doing?

She's putting a rucksack into a locker.

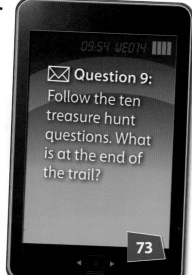

09:54 WED 14

✉ Question 9:
Follow the ten treasure hunt questions. What is at the end of the trail?

1 Listen and read. 3.36

2　Look and say. Which sentence is in the story?

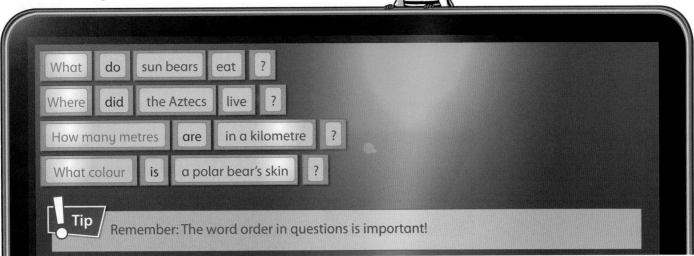

| What | do | sun bears | eat | ? |

| Where | did | the Aztecs | live | ? |

| How many metres | are | in a kilometre | ? |

| What colour | is | a polar bear's skin | ? |

! Tip Remember: The word order in questions is important!

3　Look at the pictures and finish the dialogue.

What colour is Mars?

Where do polar bears live?

How many legs has a bee got?

What did Karl Benz invent?

Class Book

4　Listen and repeat. 🔊 3.37

What colour is Mars?

Where do polar bears live?

How many legs has a bee got?

What did Karl Benz invent?

5　Choose a different picture. Make a question about it.

| Where | How many legs | What | What colour |

| do | has | did | is | live | got | invent |

| polar bears | penguins | tigers | a spider |

| a bee | a worm | Karl Benz |

| John Logie Baird | Mars | Saturn | ? |

6　Complete the grammar table.

I often go to museums in the holidays. Read the leaflets for these museums.

1 Read the texts quickly. Answer the questions.

In which museum can you see ...

horses   a school   gold   sculptures   exhibits

SOVEREIGN HILL

Gold was very important in the history of Australia. Many people from all over the world went to Australia. They worked in the gold mines and looked for gold in the streams. Sovereign Hill is a reconstruction of a gold mining town. It is a living museum with guides dressed in costume who can tell you all about life in the town in the 1850s.

You can go down into the gold mine. It was dark and dangerous in the mines. You can also try panning for gold in the stream. You have to use a big sieve to separate the sand and stones from the water. If you are lucky you will find some gold!

You can see the miners' houses, shops and schools. In those days the shop keepers often made the things they sold. You can see how they made medicines and sweets. You can try making candles for yourself. You can ride in a coach pulled by horses too!

At the end of the day you will know a lot more about gold and life in a gold mining town, and if you work hard when you are panning for gold, you may be a little richer too!

The Museum in a Box

We usually think that art is made by famous artists and that you can only see it in big art galleries. But art is just a way to communicate a thought, or experience, or feeling or opinion. So everybody can make a work of art!

The Museum in a box is a very small museum. In fact it is a box with small drawers in Karen Turner's house. There is a very small work of art in each drawer. They are made by people all over the world. Each work of art is connected to a story or a memory of the person who made them. There are pictures, collages and tiny sculptures.

Karen takes a photo of all the exhibits and puts them on the internet. When a new person sends Karen their work of art she empties one of the drawers and puts the new exhibit in its place.

2 Find these words in the text.

1 works of art with three dimensions

2 objects in an exhibition

3

4 pictures made from pieces of paper and other materials

5

6 places where people dig minerals from the ground

7

3 Read the text again and answer the questions.

1 Who worked in the gold mines in Australia?

2 What places are there in the town?

3 What can you make at Sovereign Hill?

4 How can you travel around Sovereign Hill?

5 What size is the Museum in a Box?

6 What kind of things are in the Museum in a Box?

7 Where can you see the exhibits?

8 Who are the artists?

1 **Listen and say which things they saw.** 3.43

2 **Listen again and choose the right answer.** 3.43

1 Eureka! is

  a a history museum. **b** an art gallery.
  c a children's museum.

2 When they were in the mouth, they had to

  a clean the teeth. **b** count the teeth.
  c move a tooth.

3 Adults _____ children.

  a have got more teeth than
  b haven't got more teeth than
  c have got the same number of teeth as

4 When Jack was playing football, he could

  a see his muscles. **b** see his heart.
  c see his skeleton.

5 Children _____ adults

  a have got more bones than
  b haven't got more bones than
  c have got the same number of bones as

6 They _____ a heart.

  a cleaned **b** walked into
  c heard

3 **Listen and find the missing words.** 3.44

Have you ever been to a museum?

Yes, I have.

Where did you go?

1

Who did you go with?

2

What was the best thing there?

3

Was it fun?

4

1 Sovereign Hill.   Eureka Museum.
   The Chocolate Museum.

2 My class.   My family.   My friends.

3 The horses.   The giant mouth.
   The gold mine.

4 No, it was a bit boring.   Yes, I loved it.
   It was OK.

4 **Do the role play with your partner. Choose different words.**

Nets

1 Look, listen and repeat. 🎧 3.45

2 Listen and read. 🎧 3.46

Common 3D shapes

A three-dimensional (3D) shape is a shape with height, width and depth. The sides of 3D shapes are called faces.

There are lots of different kinds of 3D shapes. We see them all around us.

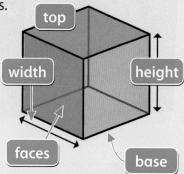

top

width

height

faces

base

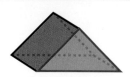

triangular prism

This is a **triangular prism**. The ends of a triangular prism are triangles. The other faces are quadrilaterals. Roofs sometimes have this shape.

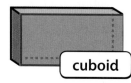

cuboid

This is a **cuboid**. A cuboid has six faces. The faces are all squares or rectangles. Bricks and boxes often have this shape.

This is a **pyramid**. The base of a pyramid can be any shape with straight sides – for example, a triangle, a square or a hexagon. The other faces are all triangles.

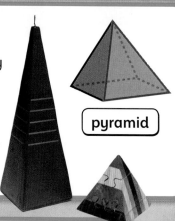

pyramid

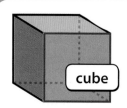

cube

This a **cube**. A cube has six faces too, but they are all exactly the same size. They are all squares. Dice and sugar lumps often have this shape.

Nets

A net is like an unfolded model of a 3D shape. This is a net of a cube. If you fold along the lines, the net makes a cube. You can draw nets on dotted or squared paper. You have to measure carefully to make sure the edges fit together.

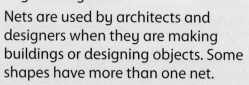

Nets are used by architects and designers when they are making buildings or designing objects. Some shapes have more than one net.

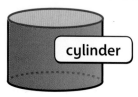

cylinder

This is a **cylinder**. The ends of a cylinder are circles. Candles, straws and paint tins are cylinders.

Words for 3D shapes

1 Look. What shapes do these nets make?

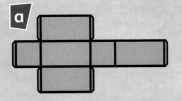  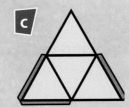 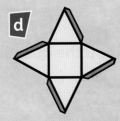

2 Read the text again and answer the questions.

1   What kind of shape is a book?
2   What kind of shape is a dice?
3   How many faces do cubes and cuboids have?
4   What kind of shape is a straw?

5   What shape is the base of a cylinder?
6   What kind of shape is a roof?
7   Do pyramids always have the same shape for a base?
8   Who uses nets?

3 Listen and say which box. 3.47

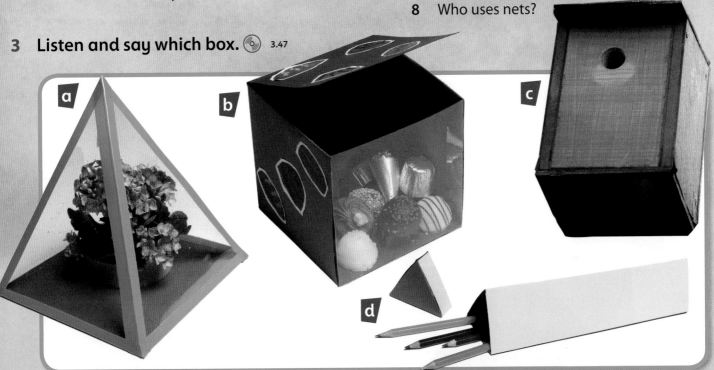

 Talk about it!

4 Talk about the boxes.

What's this box for?	
It's for a plant.	chocolates
It's a nesting box.	a pencil case
What's it made of?	
It's made of wood.	card glass plastic
What shape is it?	
It's a cuboid.	cube triangular prism pyramid

Me and my world

1 Read the questions and find the answers.

1 Where does Hakeem live?

2 Where did he go with his family?

3 Where did they stay?

4 What did they visit?

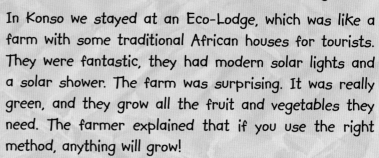

Hi, my name's Hakeem. I live in Addis Ababa, the capital of Ethiopia. It's a big city with skyscrapers, big roads, buses, and lots and lots of people. My dad works in an office in the centre, but he doesn't like the city much. He prefers the country and he's really interested in green living. That's why we went to the Konso region last year.

It took us twelve hours to drive to Konso. We saw lots of dry and dusty countryside. My dad explained that years ago there were lots of trees in Ethiopia, but people cut them down to make fires and to build houses and fields. If there were more trees, other plants would grow and there would be more animals too. In Ethiopia we have planted more than 10 billion trees – I think it's great.

In Konso we stayed at an Eco-Lodge, which was like a farm with some traditional African houses for tourists. They were fantastic, they had modern solar lights and a solar shower. The farm was surprising. It was really green, and they grow all the fruit and vegetables they need. The farmer explained that if you use the right method, anything will grow!

We visited some villages near the Eco-Lodge. There aren't many cars in Konso, people usually walk, so we did too. On the first day we went to Dokattu and met the blacksmith. He works with metal and he helped me make a knife. The next day we went to a cave with a potter and her daughters. We dug clay from the cave and then made some bowls. It wasn't easy, but it was fun! On the third day some Konso dancers came to the Lodge in the evening and we had a barbecue together. Then they taught us the local dance, and told us funny stories too. It was a brilliant end to three fantastic days.

2 Read again and answer the questions.

1 What is Addis Ababa like?
2 Why did people cut down the trees?
3 How did they go to Konso?
4 Why are people planting trees in Ethiopia?
5 What were the houses at the Eco-Lodge like?

6 Why do things grow in the Eco-Lodge farm?
7 What do blacksmiths do?
8 What do potters do?
9 What did Hakeem make?
10 What did they do on their last evening?

3 Think about it! Now discuss in groups.

Like many people, Hakeem's dad is interested in green living.

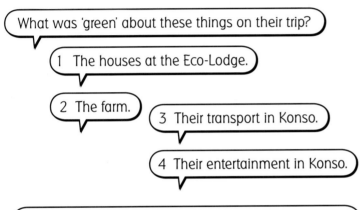

What was 'green' about these things on their trip?

1 The houses at the Eco-Lodge.

2 The farm.

3 Their transport in Konso.

4 Their entertainment in Konso.

What do you do for a greener life? Could you do more?

Learning to learn - Using ICT tools to review

You can make questionnaires and quizzes in English on your computer.

1 You can use a site to make a questionnaire and then send it to a friend, or you can put it in your blog.

2 You can download templates which help you make quizzes in English with different types of questions.

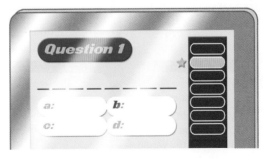

Why don't you make one about this book?

Revision

Play the game!

How to play
- Play in two teams of two.
- You need six paper counters each. **Team 1:** write *1* on your counters. **Team 2:** write *2* on your counters.
- Put a counter on the board; it must sit on top of another counter if it isn't on the bottom row.
- Follow the instructions.
- The first team to make a line of **four** is the winner.

Make a question and answer.

will / it / ? / What / do / rains / if / we / build / . We'll / shelter / a

---

Say two words with these sounds.

/eɪ/   /æ/

Complete the question.

What _____ is it?

It's a cuboid.

Say these space words.

a t_____ a m_____
an a_____ a r_____
a sp_____ sh_____

Say two words with these sounds.

/ɜː/   /ʌ/

How long would it take to travel to Mars?

Say these words for survival items.

a s_____ a k_____
a w_____ a f_____ p_____
r_____ m_____

What do pandas eat?

What colour is Mars?

Make a question.

she / if / What / had / she / do / a / phone / would?

Complete the sentences.

I' _____ _____ my whistle.

I _____ find the matches.

Say these airport words.

ch_____ in your l_____
g_____ your b_____ c_____
g_____ through s_____
s_____ your p_____

Complete the sentence.

It _____ swim well _____ it's got webbed feet.

Make a sentence.

. / If / he / , / we'll / we four / points / answer / get / find

---

Say these words for survival items.

f_____ l_____ p_____
n_____ and t_____
r_____ b_____

Complete the question.

_____ _____ , _____ the information desk?

Say the names of five planets.

Make a question.

went / What / do / if / they / the / they / moon / ? / to / would

---

Say some of the survival features of animals.

Say these space words.

an as_____ a s_____
a c_____ a m_____
a sp_____ st_____

Complete the sentences.

I _____ the answer is the car.

I agree _____ Tom.

Say these airport words.

d_____ a_____
p_____ pi_____
f_____ a_____
s_____ g_____

Say two words with these sounds.

/s/   /ʃ/

Say the words for five 3D shapes.

Where did the Aztecs live?

What colour is a polar bear's skin?

Birthdays

1 Read and find the photos.

1 Many countries celebrate birthdays with a birthday cake. There is usually one candle for each year of your life. You have to close your eyes and blow out the candles. If you blow out all the candles in one go, you can make a wish.

2 In some places in India, it is traditional for the birthday child to wear coloured clothes and take chocolates to school. They give the chocolates to their friends.

3 'The bumps' is an old birthday tradition in Britain. Your friends hold you by your arms and legs and lift you up and down while they count. If you are 12, they lift you up 13 times – once for every year of your life, and once for luck.

4 In Denmark, people sometimes put a flag outside the window when it is someone's birthday. Some people put flags on the table during birthday parties too.

5 Children in Mexico often have a 'piñata' at their birthday parties. A piñata is a model made out of paper and glue and filled with sweets and small presents. Some piñatas look like animals. You hang the piñata from the ceiling with string. Children take turns to wear a scarf round their eyes, and hit the piñata with a stick. When it breaks, they eat the sweets!

6 In some places in Canada, it is traditional to put butter on the birthday child's nose, for good luck. Butter makes your nose slippery, so bad luck can't catch you!

2 Listen and choose the right answer. 4.1

		a	b
1	Where is Anna from?	England.	Canada.
2	Where did she go swimming?	In a swimming pool.	In a lake.
3	How many friends went with her?	Two.	Three.
4	What was the weather like?	Warm and sunny.	Warm but not sunny.
5	Who threw Anna in the water?	Her friends.	Her mum and dad.
6	What did they do after the picnic?	They rode their bikes.	They played football.

Festivals of light

1 Read and find the photos.

Light and fire have always been very important to human beings and at the same time they are mysterious and difficult to understand. They often form a part of celebrations around the world.

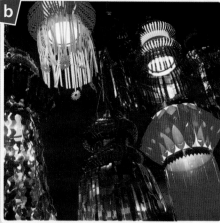

1 Candles are part of Christmas celebrations in many countries where the days in December are short and dark and the nights are long. In Sweden, St Lucia's Day on 13th December is an important part of Christmas celebrations. The oldest girl in the family is 'St Lucia' for one day. She wears a long white dress with a red belt. On her head, she wears a wreath with candles or electric lights in it. She gives everyone in the family a special cake.

2 Loi Krathong in Thailand is a very old festival of lights. It is a celebration of water. A 'krathong' is a tiny boat. Traditionally they are made of banana leaves, but you can buy or make paper ones too. People put candles and flowers in the boats, and float them in rivers. All the rivers are full of little lights! Some people believe that the krathong take away your bad luck. After this, people celebrate the festival in other ways – with fireworks, dancing and other entertainment.

3 Diwali is a very important Indian festival. It takes place in October or November, and usually lasts for about five days. The festival celebrates the victory of good over evil, and light over darkness. It is celebrated by Indian communities all around the world. 'Diwali' means 'a row of lights' and all the different Diwali traditions include lights. People decorate houses, shops and public places with little lamps, candles or electric lights. Fireworks are also a big part of the celebrations, and people give each other presents.

2 Answer the questions. Use the text to help you.

1 What does 'St Lucia' wear?

2 Who does 'St Lucia' give special cakes to ?

3 What is a 'krathong'?

4 What do people put in the krathong?

5 When does the Diwali festival take place?

6 What does 'Diwali' mean?

Carnival

1 Read.

A carnival is a big public celebration that takes place every year. There is usually music and dancing in the streets, and people dress up in special clothes. Different countries have different Carnival traditions and different names for Carnival.

Do you celebrate a carnival in your country? What is it called?

Carnevale Mardi Gras **Carnaval** **Fasnacht** Karneval Fasching

Carnival in Rio de Janeiro, Brazil, is one of the biggest carnivals in the world. It takes place in February or March, and lasts for four days. Traditionally, it is a preparation for Lent (the 40 days before Easter). Samba dancing is a very important part of Carnival. The dancers practise all year. People decorate big lorries for the parades, and they make special costumes. They look fantastic! People travel from all over the world to watch the parades.

The Carnival in Québec, in Canada, is a preparation for Lent and a celebration of the end of winter. People enjoy lots of winter activities, like dog sledding, snow sculpture, and canoe races. A huge ice palace is built every year in the middle of the town, and about 100,000 people visit it. The palace is different every year. A big snowman called Bonhomme is the mascot for the festival. He wears a red hat and a coloured belt.

The Battle of Flowers is the name of a carnival in Jersey. It takes place every August in the town of St Helier. The first Battle of Flowers took place in August 1902 when a new king was crowned in England. Big lorries are decorated with flowers, and people dress up. There is a parade in the daytime, and another parade at night. In the past, people threw flowers at each other – this is why it is called the 'Battle of Flowers'!

2 Read. Listen and match. 4.2

a This is some Samba music from the Rio carnival. I love Samba. It's fast and fun!

b I heard this music at the Battle of Flowers carnival in Jersey. It is marching music. I can hear lots of drums.

c This is traditional music that we play at the Québec carnival. We sing words about Bonhomme, the snowman.

Flyers Let's practise!

1 Look at the picture and complete the notes.

	Where is he/she?	What is he/she doing?	What does he/she look like?	What is he/she wearing?
1	next to the river		short red hair, freckles, happy	
2		watering flowers	curly blond hair, happy	orange dress, black shoes
3	next to the door			green shirt, brown trousers, yellow boots
4	sitting under a tree		long blond hair, glasses	
5		feeding ducks		white T-shirt, blue shorts, pink socks, white trainers
6		fishing	short brown hair, beard	

2 Cover the table above.

Describe a person in the picture for your partner to guess.

Listening

Listen and draw lines. There is one example. 4.3

Sally   David   Michael   Sarah

Emma   William   Richard

Flyers   Let's practise!

1 Complete the sentences with the correct form of **play**, **go** or **have**.

1   Where did you **go** in the holidays?

2   I enjoy _____ to the cinema with my friends.

3   I haven't _____ my lunch yet.

4   I would like to _____ in the football match on Saturday.

5   We were _____ in the garden when it started raining.

6   I couldn't _____ to school on Monday because I was ill.

7   I _____ skiing in Austria last January.

8   Shall we _____ tennis?

9   I'm going to _____ a burger for dinner.

10 Yesterday I _____ in the park all morning.

2 Read and match.

look/sound/smell/feel/taste + adjective:	*What's for dinner? It <u>smells</u> delicious!*
look/sound/smell/feel/taste + like + noun:	*That girl's hat <u>looks like</u> a parrot!*

1   <u>Look at my new pencil sharpener. It looks like</u>   a beautiful!

2   I didn't like that new ice cream. It tasted like   b a rubbish bin!

3   I like holding my hamster. He feels   c a racing car!

4   What's that horrible smell? It smells like   d cats fighting!

5   Can I see your new dress? Oh, it looks   e very soft.

6   Have you heard that terrible new song? It sounds like   f honey.

 # Reading & Writing

Read the story. Choose a word from the box.
Write the correct word next to numbers 1–5. There is one example.

looked	playing	ball	down
going	sounded	up	kitten
looking	went		

One day last summer I was ___**playing**___ football in our garden with my
friend Peter. Peter kicked the ball very hard and it went over the wall. I
climbed over the wall but I couldn't see the ball. While I was
(1) _____ for it, I heard a strange noise. It (2) _____ like
a baby crying. I looked up and saw a small kitten in a tree. It couldn't
climb (3) _____ and it was crying. I ran home and told my mum.
She said, "Well done, Adam. I think that's Mrs Johnson's new kitten." She
phoned Mrs Johnson.

The next morning, Mrs Johnson came to our house. She wanted to say
thank you to me for finding her (4) _____. She gave me a present.
It was a new football! I (5) _____ to Peter's house and we played
football in his garden. The new ball was great!

Now choose the best name for the story. Tick one box.

a) Adam gets a new ball ☐

b) Mrs Johnson finds a kitten ☐

c) A present for Peter ☐

Let's practise!

1 Look at the pictures below. Write words or phrases.

2 Listen and tick (✔) the box. There is one example. ◎ 4.4

What did Jane have for lunch at school?

chicken

chips

carrot

rice

A ☐   B ☐   C ✔

1 What has Jane got in her bag?

A ☐   B ☐   C ☐

2 Which man is Jane's dad?

A ☐   B ☐   C ☐

3 Where is the sports centre?

SPORTS CENTRE   SPORTS CENTRE   SPORTS CENTRE

A ☐   B ☐   C ☐

Flyers

Listening

Listen and tick (✔) the box. There is one example. 🔊 4.5

What has Mrs Smith bought?	 A ☐	 B ✔	 C ☐

1 Where should Tom put the biscuits?

 A ☐    B ☐   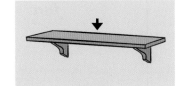 C ☐

2 What time are they going to have dinner?

 A ☐   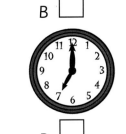 B ☐    C ☐

3 What does Tom need to get out of the cupboard?

 A ☐    B ☐   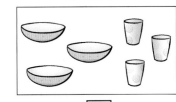 C ☐

4 What did Tom do at school today?

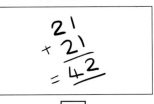 A ☐   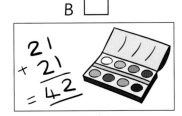 B ☐   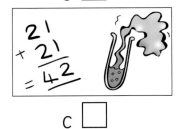 C ☐

5 What will Tom do tomorrow if it rains?

 A ☐   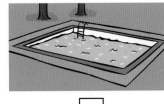 B ☐    C ☐

Flyers   Let's practise!

1 Write the phrases in the correct box. Use your dictionary.

> ~~dinner~~   ~~fun~~   ~~the shopping~~   a shower   a mess   a mistake
> your homework   a noise   an argument   the washing up
> dinner   the cooking   the bed   a good time   a list

have	do	make
fun	*the shopping*	*dinner*

2 Complete the sentences.

> after   to   out   ~~up~~   on   at   in   off   for

1 Why do I have to get __up__ early? I want to stay in bed.

2 Look _____ my picture! Do you like it?

3 I don't know where the library is but I can find _____.

4 Where's my bag? I looked _____ it upstairs but I couldn't find it.

5 It's very hot outside. Put _____ your sunhat, please.

6 Do you want to listen _____ my new CD? It's brilliant!

7 My mum is at work so I've got to look _____ my sister.

8 Turn _____ the television, please! I don't like this programme.

Reading & Writing

Read the diary and write the missing words. Write one word on each line.

Example When I got ____up____ this morning, it was snowing!

1 I _____ my breakfast, then I went outside with

2 my sister, Katy. It was very cold so we put _____

our coats, hats and gloves. We made a snowman

and it looked like my dad! Dad smiled when he saw

3 _____. Then Katy and I went inside and watched

4 a film on television. It was _____ 'The Magic

5 Island'. We had a good _____ today!

Syllabus

Unit	Grammar	Vocabulary	Functional language	'Learning through English' vocabulary and skills	Writing
1	**The Present simple and the Present continuous** What do you usually do on Saturdays? She usually plays tennis on Saturdays. What's she doing today? She's fishing in the lake.	**Nature features** a small island, a steep hill, a deep lake, a high waterfall, a dark cave, a long bridge, a wide river, a narrow stream	**How to talk about size** How long is …? How high is …? How wide is …? How deep is …? It's … metres long / high / deep / wide.	*Geography: Rivers* **River features** upper course, middle course, lower course, stream, hydroelectric plant, factory, flood plains, port • *Learn to identify parts of a river*	**Writing task:** A description of a place you know **Writing tip:** Position of adjectives
2	**The Present perfect with** *yet* **and** *already* Have you tidied your room yet? He's already eaten a toffee apple. I haven't gone on the roller coaster yet.	**Theme park words** a big wheel, a roller coaster, bumper cars, a waterslide, a merry-go-round, a bouncy castle, a prize, candyfloss, a toffee apple	**How to make and respond to suggestions** Shall we go …? Why don't we go …? How about going …? Let's have a …! OK. Good idea. No, I don't want to. No, I don't like …	*Maths: Charts and graphs* **Charts and graphs** pie chart, section, bar chart, bar, line graph, cross, pictogram, symbol • *Learn to use charts and graphs to show data*	**Writing task:** A postcard **Writing tip:** What to remember when writing a postcard
3	**The Present perfect and the Past simple** Have you been to China? He's been to Argentina. When did they go to Africa? I saw a celebrity last year.	**Airport words** check in your luggage, get your boarding card, go through security, show your passport, go to your gate, board the plane, departures, arrivals, passenger, pilot, flight attendant, security guard	**How to have a phone conversation** Hello, this is … Hi, it's … Hello, who's that? Can I speak to …, please? Sorry, … isn't here. I'll call back later. Goodbye. Bye.	*Art: Perspective in art* **Words to describe perspective** vanishing point, horizon, sight lines, foreground, background • *Learn to add depth to pictures*	**Writing task:** A story **Writing tip:** Past tense verb forms in stories
4	**The Past simple and the Past continuous** I was watching TV when the phone rang. What happened when she was talking to her dad? He hurt his knee when he was climbing a tree.	**Extreme weather words** a blizzard, heavy snow, strong winds, freezing temperatures, a heatwave, high temperatures, thunder and lightning, sunny, dry, a storm, heavy rain, dark clouds	**How to talk about changes in the weather** It's getting colder / darker. I think there's going to be a storm / blizzard. I think it's going to rain / snow.	*Science: Weather maps* **Weather features** wet, dry, hot, warm, cool, cold • *Learn to read weather maps*	**Writing task:** A weather story **Writing tip:** Useful words and phrases for stories
5	***will won't*** Will he be in Paris in June? No, he won't. I'll be at school this afternoon.	**Film set words** stuntman, reporter, bodyguard, actor, camera operator, extra, fan, director, shake hands, sign an autograph, wave	**How to describe a person** What's he like? What does he look like? He's tall / bald. He's got a moustache. I think he looks mean. He looks intelligent to me.	*History: The history of films* **Film words** camera, projector, frame, subtitle, shoot a film • *Learn about the history of films* • *Practise using a timeline*	**Writing task:** A film review **Writing tip:** Useful expressions for reviewing

Unit	Grammar	Vocabulary	Functional language	'Learning through English' vocabulary and skills	Writing
6	**must can't might could** It must be the answer. She could be in the bedroom. They can't be watching TV. He might be visiting his grandma.	**Concert words** band, drummer, guitarist, lead singer, keyboard player, drums, electric guitar, keyboards, stage, lights, speakers, microphone	**How to describe a person's experience** She's played in ten different countries. She's made three albums. She's had two number ones.	*Music: Jazz* **Music words** notes, saxophone, tune, double bass • *Learn about jazz music*	**Writing task:** A description of a school show **Writing tip:** What to include in a descriptive text: facts and opinions
7	**The First conditional** What will we do if it rains? If he's hungry, he'll go fishing.	**Survival items** shelter, knife, whistle, frying pan, rope, matches, fishing line, plasters, needle and thread, rucksack, binoculars	**How to ask about something you've lost** I can't find the … I've lost my … Have you seen the …? Have you looked in …? Why don't you check in …? It isn't there. I've found it!	*Science: Survival features* **Survival features** fur, claws, skin, tongue, webbed feet, beak • *Learn to identify animals' survival features* • *Talk about how animals adapt to their environment*	**Writing task:** A diary **Writing tip:** What to include in a diary: facts and opinions
8	**The Second conditional** What would you do if you saw an alien? If she had a lot of money, she'd travel around the world.	**Space words** star, telescope, moon, alien, rocket, space shuttle, astronaut, satellite, crater, Earth, meteorite, space station	**How to give an opinion** I think … is the answer. I'm sure it's … It could be … I agree with … I don't agree. Why? Because …	*Science: The solar system* **Planets** Mercury, Venus, Earth, Mars, Jupiter, Saturn, Uranus, Neptune • *Read tables about the planets and do calculations*	**Writing task:** A leaflet about a holiday destination **Writing tip:** Imperatives
9	**Questions** What do polar bears eat? Where did the Romans live? How many metres are in a kilometre? What colour is a crocodile? When were the last Olympics?	**Museum words** information desk, ticket office, display, stairs, lift, exit, entrance, lockers, audio guide, headphones, ground floor, first floor	**How to give and ask for directions in a building** Excuse me, where's the information desk / where are the toilets? On the ground floor. Over there on the left. Next to the shop. Opposite check in.	*Maths and Design: Nets* **Words for 3D shapes** cube, cuboid, cylinder, triangular prism, pyramid • *Learn about 3D shapes* • *Learn to identify nets*	**Writing task:** A description of a special place or time **Writing tip:** Including feelings in descriptions

OXFORD
UNIVERSITY PRESS

ACKNOWLEDGEMENTS

Main illustrations by: Maya Gavin pp.2, 3, 4, 5, 6, 7, 8, 13, 14, 15, 16 (Meg), 21, 22, 23, 24 (Ray), 31, 32, 33, 34 (Oli), 39, 40, 41, 42 (Meg), 47, 48, 49, 50 (Rav), 57, 58, 59, 60 (Oli), 65, 66, 67, 68 (Oli), 73, 74, 75 (characters), 76 (Meg)

Song artwork by: Lorena Alvarez Gomez pp.12, 20, 38, 46, 64, 72

Other illustrations by: Judy Brown pp.86, 87, 88, 89, 90, 91, 92, 93; William Donohoe pp.10, 11, 44, 70; Christiane Engel (Good Illustration) p.27; Celia Hart pp.28, 54, 80; John Haslam pp.30, 56, 82; Jan McCafferty pp.24 (Daedalus), 26; Andy Parker p.68 (Space Tour); Mark Ruffle pp.78, 79; Jo Taylor (Sylvie Poggio Artists Agency) p.75; Dave Whamond (3 in a Box) pp.9, 16, 24, 34, 36, 42, 50, 52, 60, 62, 69, 76

Cover illustration by: Maya Gavin

Commissioned photography: Gareth Boden pp.43, 78, 79, 83

The Publishers would also like to thank the following for their kind permission to reproduce photographs and other copyright material: Alamy pp.8 (Claire Noakes/Whit Richardson), (accident victim being put on stretcher/Ashley Cooper), (Jenny Brown/David R. Frazier Photolibrary, Inc.), 10 (hydroelectric plant/WoodyStock), 11 (water sports/StockShot), (bridge/David Robertson), (tractor/Marc Hill), 16 (London Eye pod/Alex Segre), (London Eye/Hideo Kurihara), (Eden project biomes/Adrian Davies), 17 (pig sculpture/Geodigital), (bee sculpture/Ashley Cooper), 25 (hangglider/David Wall), (parachutist/David Wall), 34 (tornado/A. T. Willett), 35 (girls building snowman/Daniel Dempster Photography), (cars buried in snow/Joe Outland), (house buried in snow/Nordicphotos), 37 (lightning/Dale O'Dell), (clouds/Deco), (park under snow/Andy Levin), (people with umbrellas/Andrew Fox), (sunshine on coast/James Osmond), 45 (Snow White/Moviestore Collection Ltd), 50 (Stomp/Theatrepix), 50 (Stomp: theatre exterior/Lenscap), 52 (slaves singing in fields/North Wind Picture Archives), (people playing jazz in room/Lebrecht Music and Arts Photo Library), 54 (bridge/Peter Barritt), (harp/Joseph Clemson), (parade/The Photolibrary Wales), (children/Topix), 61 (snake/Shaun Cunningham), (driftwood fire/Mediacolors), (hut on beach/Paul Prescott), 62 (polar bear/Arco Images GmbH), (sun bear with protruding tongue/Vova Pomortzeff), (sun bear main pic/Arco Images GmbH), 63 (golden eagle/Willridge Images), (snowy owl/Maximilian Weinzierl), (hummingbird/Bob Gaspari), 77 (dinosaur/Kevin Schafer), 80 (plant nursery/Richard Human), 83 (pinata/Danita Delimont), (Danish house/Heini Kettunen), 84 (Krathong/The Photolibrary Wales), (Christmas/Chad Ehlers), 85 (Bonhomme/Rubens Abboud); Ardea p.61 (beetles/Ken Lucas); Corbis pp.10 (factory/Ashley Cooper), 11 (port/Richard Cummins), 28 (suspension bridge/Radius Images), 35 (skier in street/David Turnley), 44 (Fred Ott's Sneeze/Corbis), 50 (Stomp/Horst Ossinger/dpa), 51 (Stomp: bins/Fernando Alvarado/EPA), (Stomp: brushes/Angel Medina G./EPA), 53 (Duke Ellington Orchestra/Bettmann), (Ella Fitzgerald/Hulton-Deutsch Collection), 62 (polar bear's claws/W. Perry Conway), 76 (panning for gold/Dave G. Houser), 77 (giant heart/Sandy Felsenthal), 85 (Battle of Flowers/James L. Amos); Eureka Museum p.77 (Eureka mouth); Fortean Picture Library p.34 (ball lightning/Werner Burger); Fotolia p.28 (Abel Tasman Park/Tupungato), (kayaks/lilufoto); Getty Images pp.17 (giant lily pads/AFP), (durian fruit/ImageMore Co. Ltd.), 29 (class discussion group/Ragnar Schmuck), 34 (teen girl/Kaz Mori/Photographer's Choice), (teen boy/Hans Neleman/Taxi), 52 (jazz club/Nat Farbman/Time & Life Pictures), 55 (class discussion group/Ragnar Schmuck), 61 (palm tree/Stuart Westmorland/Riser), (fish on cloth/Bertrand Gardel/hemis.fr), 62 (sun bear up tree/AFP), 81 (class discussion group/Ragnar Schmuck), 85 (Rio carnival/Vanderlei Almeida); iStock pp.29 (dog/dageldog), 80 (African boy/MissHibiscus), (dry African landscape/Guenter Guni); The Kobal Collection pp.42 (Shrek/DreamWorks LLC), 44 (The Great Train Robbery/Edison), 45 (The Wizard of Oz/MGM), (The Jazz Singer/Warner Bros); Melat Negash p.80 (Eco-Lodge/Melat Negash); Rex Pictures pp.8 (mountain rescue team posing/Michael Dunlea), 16 (Alton Towers ride/Sonny Meddle), 42 (Jungle Book/W. Disney/Everett), 50 (Stomp/Ken McKay/ITV), 53 (Fats Waller/Everett Collection), (Miles Davis/Images), (Charlie Parker and Dizzie Gillespie/Everett Collection); Shutterstock pp.7, 33, 41, 49, 59, 67, 75 (boy with computer/Michal Bednarek), 25 (hot-air balloon/Sonya Etchison), 28 (girl with towel/bikeriderlondon), 55 (girl with horse/Terrie L. Zeller), 63 (penguins/Neale Cousland); Science Photo Library p.77 (X-ray/D. Roberts); Topfoto pp.45 (Little Nemo/TopFoto), 84 (Diwali/Dinodia)